SHADER

99 Notes on Car Washes, Making Out in Church, Grief, and Other Unlearnable Subjects

BY **DANIEL NESTER**

99: THE PRESS
San Francisco, California
Lowell, Massachusetts
2015

This is a work of memory, and though I have done my best to tell a story that is true, there will be times when my bias and flaws show themselves. I have done my best to research and clarify facts and dates, and have interviewed others for their perspectives. Except for direct blood relatives, all names and some personal details have been changed. These are Notes, incomplete and temporary, in the hope they add up to something complete. There came a moment quite recently when I realized I'm not finished with the past, not yet. I live warily and happily with former versions of myself, which I think of as long-lost friends who sometimes arrive at my door the middle of the night with a bottle of wine. There also came another moment when I realized that, though I may not make for a very good protagonist, I'm all I've got. Another thing I've realized is that, no matter what happens, no matter where I go, there's a part of me that remains a Shader.

FIRST EDITION

Designed by Colleen Cole. The astronomical image on the cover was photographed by NASA, ESA, and M. Livio and the Hubble 20th Anniversary Team (STScI). *Hubble Captures View of 'Mystic Mountain.'* Feb. 1–2, 2010. Carina Nebula, HubbleSite Gallery.

Library of Congress Cataloging-in-Publication Data has been applied for.

ISBN: 9780988266254

The pure products of America
go crazy—

—William Carlos Williams, "To Elsie"

Contents

ACT ONE

ACT TWO

ACT THREE

ACT ONE

1.

Notes on a Prologue:
The Shattered Bridge

April 2012: Upstate New York—I hold the phone up to my face to film two girls on a tiny screen. Our daughters, five and three years old, woke up demanding attention, demanding to be taken care of, and have commenced bouncing on the bed. My wife tries to settle them down. I hold the phone steady.

"Repeat after me: 'I am having a wonderful childhood.' "

They say it, huffing, the younger one trails behind a syllable or two.

"Now say, 'You're a great dad.' "

I confirm the clip is saved and look up. I wonder if they will remember.

• • •

December 2012: Upstate New York—I sit on the couch, laptop attached to my thighs, and scramble to grade the last of my students' papers. The girls sit next to me and watch *Dora the Explorer,* spellbound.

To a sleep-deprived adult, *Dora the Explorer* feels like a dream or hallucination, one butterfly ball or tiara party after another. In our house, Dora's voice signals the end of the day. While dinner cooks on the stove in the kitchen, in the other room unicorns are rescued, magical mirrors run into, and mermaids are lost and found.

This episode of *Dora the Explorer* is called "Te Amo." A mean magician has cast a spell, and Dora and her friends must fix a Shattered Bridge to get to the other side. To do this, they must scream "Te amo," *I love you*, at the top of their lungs.

"Te amo! Te amo!" the girls shout, still sucking their thumbs.

I shout with them. "Te amo! Te amo!"

"Stop being silly," Miriam, the older girl, says to me, scolding.

"Yeah," Beatrice, the younger girl, chimes in. "Stop being silly!"

"All right," I say. "I'll stop."

The Shattered Bridge gets fixed.

2.

Notes on a Prologue,
with Cameo from Billy Squier

Some hot July nights, the air itself seems eager for the day to end. This was such a night, in 2013, on the South Shore of Long Island.

My wife's mother lives in a 200-year-old farmhouse on the outskirts of Bellport. We arrived that night in time for a swim, a late supper, and an abbreviated story time with our daughters. The pool filter hummed in the yard. I grew restless.

• • •

I have tricked out my car with a stereo that is so loud it is capable of shaking the rearview mirror. I installed a subwoofer, precision-made tweeters, and an amplifier with 300 watts of digital power because I have my own car after 20 years without one. I also did it because, since entering middle age, I need a sanctuary to blast music and drown out the distorted thoughts that preoccupy my mind. The stereo is loaded with sentimental pop, power ballads, hardcore punk, Schubert lieder. Inside the car, I am 17 again. Inside the car, I blast music and sing along.

I thought about going out for a drive.

• • •

I turned on the TV. A commercial for a rock festival announced that Billy Squier was set to play in two hours.

Billy Squier! I have fucking loved Billy Squier since eighth grade. He was a friend of the members of Queen, my favorite rock band, which has always been a bonus. Even without that connection, I regarded Billy Squier as the American T. Rex, the way he made hard rock sound like pop and pop sound like hard rock. From the day I heard "The Stroke" pop out of the speakers on my FM radio, I was hooked.

Thirty years later, Billy Squier qualified as a genuine recluse. His post-"Stroke" story goes like this: a rock star on top of the world has a flop video, then disappears. "Rock Me Tonite," a 1984 synth-heavy single infamous for its unintentionally camp video, drives Squier to pull a Syd Barrett and drop out of the music business.

I don't remember it quite that way, but the video *was* pretty bad: Squier sports a shoulder-cut *Flashdance* shirt and writhes around on pink satin sheets. People at the time called it "Cock Me Tonite." The thing is, Squier didn't quit; he kept at it for more than a decade, and I remained a loyal fan. Lots of people still loved him. It was only after Squier put out an acoustic album in 1998 that he truly went off the radar.

There were hints of what he was up to. If you picked up a free flyer from Gotham Writers Workshop in New York City, you'd read a blurb from "singer and songwriter" Billy Squier raving about the draft of a screenplay he completed taking classes there. Other than the occasional solo gig announced on his website, not much was going on.

I got in my car and followed the GPS lady's directions.

• • •

Hands down, it was the worst organized show I've ever attended. I have been to arena shows with bathrooms six inches deep in water, where women used urinals standing on buckets. I have seen skinheads form chains to keep teenagers inside mosh pits. I have slept on dirt at a folk festival where the only available food was a dry vegan sheetcake. This gig seemed designed to fall apart. There were no signs to anything, anywhere. People were anxious to see the full lineup of bands, waiting in a ticket line that went down the block.

. . .

Billy Squier opened the evening part of the festival. I heard his first song, "In the Dark," while still waiting in line. I spotted a couple people in Billy Squier t-shirts behind me, shaking their heads. As soon as I got my ticket, I bolted past the fried bread trucks and Deadhead trinket stands, broke through the beer line, and navigated around picnic blankets that held people's spots for when the Doobie Brothers went on.

And there he was: Billy Squier! He was doing "She's a Runner," a fave ballad from *Emotions in Motion*. I clapped along with the hundred or so people standing in front of the stage.

And then he did a song from his acoustic album, *Happy Blue*. I bought it when it came out, but didn't listen to it that much. "I'm going to play 'The Pursuit of Happiness,'" he said. "It's from an album that went nowhere."

He seemed kind of sad. I resolved to listen to the song, give it my full attention, rather than make off to get a beer or check my email. This time the song sounded different. He was playing on an acoustic, but it was loud and distorted. He knocked behind the neck and let the open strings feed back.

. . .

Most people I know nowadays would think the song is cheesy, or think Billy Squier is cheesy. Most people look to music to val-idate their tastes, rather than simply react to what they hear. Whatever. After he sang "If you want love/you gotta love some-body/If you wanna be happy/stand in line," I was on the verge of tears. In my memory now, I feel some weight lifted from my chest as he played it.

This all sounds like a cheap epiphany scene from a bad film. I know this.

• ◆ •

He left the stage abruptly. The sound guy was probably asleep, and so he didn't turn down his guitar before Billy Squier unplugged it. It sounded a *ka-chung* across the crowd. The set was short. It was a rock festival and all, with different acts and a couple of stages, but it seemed like he was on stage for only a half hour. Who cares, I thought. I got to see Billy Squier. He had opened for Queen in 1982 when I was 14. My mother wouldn't let me go without an escort. To finally see him 30 years later felt like one door shutting and another opening.

No way was I going to stay for what came next, some Doobie Brothers bullshit. I posted photos to share my joy, then got lost trying to leave. At one point, I stood under an empty tent closed in on three sides. A teenaged security guard talked to some girls through the fence.

• ◆ •

On the ride home, I kept the stereo off. The voice of the GPS lady led me back to my mother-in-law's house. My cell phone rang. It was my sister. She usually texts me because I never answer my phone. So I answered.

She was crying. Sobbing. My sister never cries. I asked her what was wrong.

She kept sobbing.

. . .

I thought about Charlie, my nephew and her oldest son, who fancied himself the Longboard Magellan of South Jersey, skating beside highways and inside stadium parking lots. Maybe he'd gotten in some disfiguring accident. I thought of my middle nephew, Johnny, in remission five years from brain cancer and rounds of chemo. His annual tests were up. And I thought of our mother, her pack-a-day habit since we were young, each X-ray miraculously unmarred by dark lungs. It was Mom. Mom was sick. I braced myself.

"Dad died," she said. "He died."

I pulled the car over. It wasn't relief I felt. It also wasn't shock. Instead, I asked practical questions, the when, the how, the why. The turn signal ticked. Patchogue traffic whooshed by.

. . .

I drove the rest of the way back, again in silence, no stereo, no voice to give me direction.

3.

Notes on Maple Shade

In the small hours of June 12, 1950, two black males from Crozer Theological Seminary in Chester, Pennsylvania, went out for a ride in the country with their dates. They pulled off Route 73 in Maple Shade, New Jersey, and stopped at Mary's Café on Main Street. It was 12:45 a.m. They sat down to be served. The waitress ignored them. The two men walked up to the bar and ordered four beers. Ernest Nichols, a German immigrant and the bar's owner, stood behind the counter. The "best thing," he said, "would be for you to leave." They refused, and sat back down at their table. This incensed Nichols.

"I want you out of here!" he shouted. Nichols then took out a pistol from under the bar; other accounts say it was a shotgun. "I'd kill for less!"

He chased them out to the parking lot. He fired into the roof; other accounts say he shot into the South Jersey sky. The four left, frightened, then got angry, and drove down Main Street to the Maple Shade police station to file a complaint, which all four signed: Pearl E. Smith and Doris Wilson, who listed their occupations as teacher and policewoman, along with the two young seminarians from Pennsylvania: Walter R. McCall and Martin Luther King, Jr.

• • •

They returned to the bar with the police and Nichols was arrested. The Camden chapter of the NAACP filed suit. The case

8

was dismissed three months later, however, when witnesses at the bar—three white Penn students—refused to testify after pressure from their parents.

• • •

Some biographers categorize the incident in Maple Shade as an epiphany for the 21-year-old King, as much of a formative influence on his teachings of direct action as when he visited Gandhi's birthplace in 1959 and developed a belief in nonviolent resistance. A few designate Mary's Café as the birthplace of the modern civil rights movement in America.

• • •

From ages 2 to 19, I lived in "The Shade," as we called it, 3.8 square miles on the southern end of Burlington County, nine miles from Philadelphia, a "suburban community located between two large shopping malls," the town's Historical Society brochure reads. Maple Shade was and remains a working-class town hemmed in by larger, richer towns—new-money communities Cherry Hill and Mount Laurel have median household incomes well above 50 percent more than Maple Shade's, old-money Moorestown more than double. There are other blue-collar areas in South Jersey—Gloucester, Vineland, parts of Camden and Pennsauken—but perhaps because of its location, Shaders are especially leery of outsiders. *There's a carload of dudes from Cinnaminson at the custard stand,* an older boy would say as he smoked cigarettes on Steinhauer Hill. *Let's go beat the shit out of them!*

Between Main Street and Forklanding Road, its delis and sub shops, barbers and bakeries, churches and baseball fields, Shaders kept to themselves.

Sundays after mass in 1950, the same summer King and his friends were thrown out of Mary's Café, my grandparents went on drives from their house in Northeast Philadelphia. My mother told my sister and me the story of how, as a three year old, she sat in the backseat with her grandmother and crossed the Tacony-Palmyra Bridge, past Camden, past what is now Palmyra and Cinnaminson, to look at houses in Maple Shade Township, just formed in 1947. To their left and right, they saw farms and forest for miles. They looked out onto peach orchards and dairy farms, out of which quarter-acre plots would be carved for small houses, and called this land "God's Country."

4.

Notes on the Circumstances Surrounding My Conception

I was conceived on the evening of June 3, 1967, the day Patricia Ann Little, who turned 19 that same day, and Michael Nester, still 18, were married at Our Lady of Perpetual Help church in Maple Shade.

◆ ◆ ◆

Eighteen months earlier, Mike Nester had finished his senior year at Bisbee High School in Bisbee, Arizona. The day he got his diploma, he walked downtown to enlist in the Navy. He was 18 and he wanted to see the world. His first change-of-station orders landed him in the exotic locale of the Philadelphia Navy Yard.

As he walked down Walnut Street one afternoon with another seaman recruit class E-1, Mike Nester spotted a six-foot-tall, skinny blonde on a cigarette break with a coworker outside Penn Mutual Insurance Company. That blonde, 18-year-old Patti Little, sported a new pixie hairstyle she called an "avocado," an update of her high school beehive.

The sailors saluted them. As my mother described it, it sounded like a scene from a Broadway musical.

◆ ◆ ◆

The four grabbed coffee and pie at a diner after work, and at one point, Mike put his palm on Patti's thigh under the table.

"He was getting fresh," she told me. "So I forked him."

"You what?" I asked.

"I stuck a fork in him. Under the table."

Her fork "drew a little blood" through Mike's dress blues. He still asked her out, and Patti gave him a fake phone number. Mike Nester proceeded to call every Little household in South Jersey, asking for Patti. "It was all very romantic," she remembers now, blushing a bit. When he finally found the right Patti Little, and Mike Nester asked her out, Patti said yes.

◆ ◆ ◆

The sailor took the bus out to Maple Shade from the city. Their dates took place in the Littles's kitchen, or they borrowed Patti's father's car and went to see a movie and neck. Patti's younger sisters, Chrissy and Terry, 8 and 10, thought he was The Most Handsome Man They've Ever Seen, and used every excuse to go to the kitchen—iced tea, ice cubes, cookies.

He looks like Elvis Presley, Chrissy said to Terry, *with his blue eyes, the pompadour!*

And those lips, those big big lips! Terry said back.

Their older sister scolded them, told them to *get lost.*

◆ ◆ ◆

According to the *Old Farmer's Almanac,* June 3, 1967, was a perfect spring day: the sky was cloudless, with a high temperature of 82 degrees and a low of 54.

After the reception, held in my grandparents' house at 20 Mecray Lane, the just-married couple began their 280-mile journey to their new apartment in Ocean View, VA, where Mike Nester was to serve out his Navy enlistment. Instead of driving through the night, they stopped at The Mallard Inn, 15 miles away from my grandparents' backyard, in Marlton, NJ. And that's where I was conceived.

Each time she has told this story over the years, my mother has gone out of her way to point out that was the night their marriage was consummated.

• • •

The Mallard Inn has long been demolished. It caught fire one windy night in 1979. The roof disappeared so quickly, one news story says, that all the tables in the dining room still had place settings, like nothing had happened.

Whenever I drive home, I get off Exit 4 of the Turnpike and turn past where I was conceived. Each time, I point to the exact spot where my mother's body met my father's body for the first time. It's just a vacant lot, a tangle of off-ramps and curbs overtaken by goldenrod, dog shit, and blue vervain.

Notes on Two First Memories, Mostly in the Present Tense

Late 1971. Mom calls us over and shows me a broken baby bottle. My sister and I kick around ivy and twigs in the back of my grandparents' yard. I am three years old; my sister, Meri, is two. My hair is blond in a side part, and I wear denim overalls almost every day. Pieces of the broken baby bottle glisten in twilight. I look down at the glass, the rubber nipple, then up at Mom's eyes, her skinny frame stooped over my face.

You can't drink from a bottle anymore, she says. From now on I have to use *big people glasses.* Low branches brush against my thighs.

I thought I broke the bottle and was being scolded. But it was a trick.

My mother was 22, had two kids, one year and one week apart. *Catholic twins,* we used to say. Meri drank from glasses already, while I still clung to the bottle, still loved the squeaks the rubber nipple made in the gap in my front teeth. So my mother dreamt up a ruse. *It was time,* she said.

She denied this ever happened for years. Baby Bottlegate remained a figment of my dramatic imagination. That's the word assigned to me, *dramatic.* Most children are dramatic, but my level of drama, according to my family, ranked as especially prone to hand-on-forehead, woe-is-me fits of distress. I could turn from tranquil to tantrum in seconds. To calm down, I'd nuzzle the crease of my elbow, smell skin and soft hair, hum in the forearm until it got wet from breath. I still perform this self-soothing, only not in public.

⋄ ⋄ ⋄

A few months later, 1972. My father takes me to see *2001: A Space Odyssey*. *You'll get to see monkeys*, he promises.

The theater goes dark. Sound fills the room—deep, then high, then screechy. I start to cry and hold on to Dad's arm.[1] I get up in my seat. Dad stretches his right arm over my chest to keep me in place. *The monkeys are coming*, he says. The music stops. The sun comes up. Quiet again.

The monkeys come, but they aren't cartoons and they're not friendly. They squat and squeal and bare their teeth, wave arms and growl at each other. A cheetah leaps from a rock and rips a monkey's body apart. I cry.

In the next scene, a monkey wakes up to a black rock outside the cave. He looks at a bone, picks it up, and starts beating the ground. Richard Strauss's one-octave fanfare *Also Sprach Zarathustra* swells up. The monkey screams, breaks more bones.

Watch, Dad tells me. *He's going to make a discovery.*

A monkey picks up a bone, then beats up another monkey. I start to cry again, breathing into my arm.[2]

---

1   What I heard was the eight-minute overture, György Ligeti's *Atmosphères*, which plays to a black screen. A composer friend explained to me that the piece is one big *cluster chord*, every note along five octaves played by the instruments of a large orchestra.

2   Streaming *2001* on my laptop forty years later, my wife makes fun of the scene. "They're people in cheap suits," she says. "How on earth did this scare you?"

   "They scared the living crap out of me," I tell her, a little louder than usual.

   As I write this, our oldest daughter is four years old. She can't even make it through *Peter Pan* or *Beauty and the Beast* without losing her shit in full-voiced yelps of fear. *So this is where psychotherapy comes from*, I think. Even fellow parents of the same young child can't listen to childhood fears with a straight face.

. . .

In many ways, these memories sum up each parent's approach: a mother fibs to help the house run efficiently, a father teaches lessons about civilization as dramatized by homicidal monkeys.

Back then, I kept asking, *what's going on?*

And I will now put into quotations what I remember him saying, his exact words, Dad's first lesson passed on to me.

"I'm seeing the same thing you're seeing."

Notes on the South Jersey Accent

"Repeat after me." My father bounces his hands in the air like an orchestra conductor. He leans forward from the edge of his chair. He's wearing his work boots and a clean workshirt, and he smells like Old Spice. "Cool, clear, *water*."

"Coo-ull, clee-ur, *wooder*."

He says it again. "Cool, clear, *water*."

We nod at the beginning of each word.

"Coo-ull, clee-ur, *wooder*."

"*No*," he says. "That's not how you say it. Pronounce each word, slowly and distinctly." His overblown diction made us giggle. We feel like contestants on a game show. "Again," he says. "Cool, clear, water."

"Coo-ull, clee-ur, *wooder*." Even *wooder*-ier than before.

"Someday, you will both speak standard English, like regular white people," he says. "Just not today."

•   •   •

The first time Dad did this, I was nine and my sister was eight. My hair was still parted in the middle and feathered down the sides, and my sister clung to her Raggedy Ann doll. Mike Nester was raising two South Jersey-accented kids, and his Henry Higgins accent reduction lessons couldn't stop it.

. . .

The South Jersey-Philadelphia regional accent remains arguably the most grating and distinctive and least imitable dialect in the English language. Actually, let's not argue about this. Ask anyone to do a *Lawn Guyland* accent or a charming Southern drawl, and that person will approximate it. Same goes for a Texas twang or a Valley Girl *totally omigod*.

Philly-South Jersey patois is harder. No vowel escapes diphthongery; no hard consonant is safe from a mid-palate dent. Extra syllables pile up so as to avoid inconvenient tongue contact or mouth closure. If you forget to listen closely, the Philadelphia accent sounds like mumbled Mandarin without the tonal shifts.

. . .

Some dialects can be transcribed and approximated, but the Philly-South Jersey accent really must be heard to be believed. You—pronounced "yew-ooh"—do not "go to the Acme to get some bottled water and soda"; you *gew ta tha Acca-me ta git sum boddled woodah and sewda*. Or you *gew to Wawa's ta buoy a hewgie*. Philadelphia is not Philadelphia; it is *Filelfia,*[3] and you root for the *Iggles* during football season.

. . .

I once wrote an article that lamented the absence of my native accent in movies. No one speaks like a Shader in movies, I wrote; no one speaks like a Shader on TV. Sports talk, sure. But not one actor has ever imitated or portrayed the Broad Street brogue on film. Not even those who come from this area: Bruce Willis, Kevin Bacon, Bradley Cooper. You can hear it in their voices, echoes of

---

3 Alternate spelling: *Fluffya.*

it, but they never speak the way they spoke when they were kids or before accent training took over.

· · ·

There was a study recently about how the Philadelphia accent has changed; *shifted* was the word the linguists used. There's still an accent, they wrote, but it's not the same one as before. The way I interpret it, which is perhaps simplistic, is the accent I grew up with is now gone. I can't hear again how people talked when I was small.

· · ·

This is how I spoke. I can still detect a South Jersey twang from across a bar. I tried my best to change my accent, but my palate just couldn't cooperate. Whenever I pass Exit 5, the Ts softens into Ds, the vowel trapezoid rounds its corners along Forklanding Road, back to its Shader formation.

7.

Notes on OLPH

OLPH, Our Lady of Perpetual Help, one of the seven titles for our Holy Mother.

Also: Old Ladies Prison Home, Old Ladies Playing Hockey, Old Ladies Pizza Hut.

Also: six square blocks along Main Street and Fellowship Road.

. . .

When you're a 12-year-old boy, there's nothing more fun than messing with nuns. At OLPH, the nuns messed with us. The Sisters of Saint Joseph, housed in a barracks-style convent across a blacktop lot, ran a tight post-Vatican II ship. Sister Barbara, a capo clamped so high up her acoustic guitar's fret board it sounded like a mandolin, led us in song as Sister Kathleen Dolan, our imperious principal, marched down the church aisle, the back of her left hand metronome-slapping the palm of her right.

Slap slap slap slap *I am the bread of life,* slap slap, *he who comes to me shall not hunger,* slap slap.

. . .

We threw tennis balls against brick walls and one another until it hit some teacher's car. A bell signaled us to line up, and I yanked a plaid tie out of a pocket, threw the ribbon around a yellow collar, clipped it just to the side of my Adam's apple, *snap,* and stepped past the metal doors into the warm insides of the brick building.

• • •

I once spent an afternoon trying to describe the breath of nuns. *You felt embalmed in their presence,* a friend once told me.

• • •

I hesitate to call OLPH an oasis because Maple Shade isn't like a desert. It's a town that resists metaphor. I did love how the school, church, convent and rectory, the whole complex, felt like a second home. We were brought in as little children, and we left as big children.

• • •

The last time I drove past Our Lady of Perpetual, I saw a boy swing from the rope on the flagpole, a human tetherball over South Poplar Avenue. An American flag dipped under his weight. Not a nun in sight. Classmates piñata-poked him each way, and the boy's face announced joy and danger as his shoes skimmed the blacktop to slow down.

I turned right, off Main Street, onto Fellowship Avenue. In front of the Sub Shoppe, two eighth-grade girls, hunched over in plaid skirts, stood in a corner, turned away from the wind. One lit a cigarette, and shared it with the other.[4]

---

4 Perhaps reaching for too much meaning, I included this sentence in previous drafts: "It reminded me, for a moment, of something sacred."

8.

Notes on the Nester Family

For 20 years, Mike Nester considered himself a Westerner in Exile. "There's no sky here," he said, as he strained to see stars, any stars, through a telescope in Maple Shade's streetlight-filled sky.

. . .

By 1970, Patti and Mike, both 23, moved back to Maple Shade. They rented a house on Germantown Avenue and had two kids to feed; my father was out of the Navy and out of a job. Finally he got a lead on a union trucking job from Eddie Kentball, a neighbor and friend of the family. The interview took place on the dock. Mike Nester lied to the steward, said *of course I know how to drive a truck*, and was hired. On his first day, he pulled his rig into a parking lot to practice. Trying to figure out the truck's ten forward gears and two in reverse, he called Patti from a pay phone, crying, frustrated. *I can't do it, I can't do it.*

. . .

For the next 12 years, Mike Nester worked the docks, loaded up trucks and drove local freight deliveries as a Teamster for the Buffalo-based Boss-Linco Lines, Inc. at its depot just north of Philadelphia. He got paid four dollars an hour—about $23, adjusted for inflation, or $47,000 a year with benefits. "Big bucks back then," Mom tells me now.

Low guys on the seniority list get night work on the docks—4 p.m. to midnight—brutal, back-breaking work, 40-pound boxes dead-lifted off the floor, 55-gallon drums bear-hugged and rolled onto dollies. On weekends, Meri walked barefoot on his back, gymnast-on-a-balance-beam-style, pops and cracks accompanying each step.

♦ ♦ ♦

Once you get past Harrisburg, Mike Nester would say, *you're back in America.* I listened to stories about Arizona, eager to hear reasons why I didn't belong in The Shade, that like him, I lived in a place unsuitable to my character. Why Dad drew the Real America line west of the Susquehanna River was never clear, but I took him at his word.

♦ ♦ ♦

Michael Nester was born in 1947 in the Panama Canal Zone, the son of Dr. Murlin Blanford Nester, a family doctor educated at Seventh-Day Adventist colleges in Kansas and California. Dr. Nester's father, Michael, the sheriff of Marshall County, Kansas, came to America with his family in 1878, "natives of Württemberg and descendants of old and honorable German ancestry," according to the *Kansas Cyclopedia*. Dr. Nester treated workers for the American Panama Canal Company at Coco Solo Hospital on the Atlantic side. There is evidence of a stint at a Georgia military base, and he is listed as a founding faculty member of a hospital in Knoxville, Tennessee. He met his second wife, Mary Ellen Fife, in nearby Maryville, Tennessee, while still married to his first, Stella.

· · ·

It's easy to imagine why the good doctor was tempted by Miss Fife's charms. A picture of my grandmother has her posed on a rock in a one-piece bathing suit as part of the court of Miss Tennessee, 1941. Their marriage announcement ran in the April 25, 1942, issue of *The Journal of the American Medical Association*.

· · ·

Their time in Panama was by all accounts prosperous. Dr. Nester brought his pregnant wife and their five-year-old daughter. After he was born, little Michael was taken care of by a black domestic who fed him plantains throughout the day. One day the chubby kid fell asleep perched under the kitchen cabinet, banana peels draped over him. They went to market in the mornings, and he started to learn Spanish.[5]

One night, a Panamanian broke into the house and stole some jewelry. Until the family left in 1952, Dr. Nester slept with a revolver under his pillow.

· · ·

After the Nesters moved to Tucson, Murlin went into private practice as a family physician. Recently my mother referred to my grandfather as a "country doctor," the kind who traded chickens for treatment. An oft-repeated story was about a rough motorcycle dude whose penis was cut off in an accident and was subsequently reattached by Dr. Nester. The household received a Christmas card with a sincere note from this man every year.

---

5 Whatever he learned didn't stick; all the Spanish he ever taught me was a Mexican 7-Up commercial—*La comida? El tenedor. El refresco?* 7-UP!—and the phrase for "your whore mother fucks donkeys."

My father's mother was described as "troubled" by my parents growing up. That's the word used. *Troubled,* and she had a smooth, Southern drawl. She was an undiagnosed manic-depressive and schizophrenic, my mother told me: "She experienced psychotic episodes."

At some point in Tucson—1961 or 1962, my mother doesn't know exactly when—the Nesters's marriage went sour. Growing up, I heard Murlin described as a distant husband. In a photo dated 1962, Dr. Nester stands in a stream, pant legs folded up, barefoot. With a tuft of gray hair on a square Nester head, he resembles the Bond villain Auric Goldfinger, except he's smiling, holding up a freshwater fish on a hook.

• • •

Both Nester grandparents died before I was born. Mary Ellen died in 1968, though there is no record for this anywhere. My father took a loan from the Navy to pay for her funeral, and my parents lived on half an enlisted seaman's salary for a year to pay it back. Dr. Nester died in Tucson on February 16, 1966. A short obituary in the June 1966 issue of *Arizona Doctor* reports that he died of "terminal pneumonia following cerebrovascular incident" after a long illness.

"Membership in the American Medical Association, Pima County Medical Society and Tennessee State Medical Association was not accompanied by political ambition," it reads, "since he was too busy caring for his many patients who will long remember him for his untiring devotion."

"The south side of Tucson has lost a good friend as well as a physician."

. . .

My dad considered himself a Westerner in Exile. But exiled why? Each question I asked him led to another question. Nights outside, Dad and I took turns looking through the telescope, up at Jupiter, its red swirls just visible in the South Jersey sky. We talked about how small we were in the universe, how very, very small.

"So, my son, what did you do today to justify you existence in the universe?"

He liked to ask unanswerable questions like this until the day he left. I could never provide an adequate answer.

Notes on Magic Music

Nothing can expunge from the record that the first album I ever bought was the Village People's *Cruisin'*. I know this, and yet hold out hope I can spin this in a positive light.

· · ·

I loved "Y.M.C.A." Who didn't? Oh, you didn't? I loved it so much that, after buying "Y.M.C.A." on 45, I bought the Village People's complete, album-length statement.

· · ·

I rode my bike to Peaches, a record store chain owned by Moonies. There in front was the cutout display: "If you think 'Macho Man' was hot, wait till you start *Cruisin'*."

Cruisin' was hot, very hot, and enjoyed by this narrator, all 38-plus minutes of it, multiple plays accompanied by crotch thrust dance routines in a darkened bedroom.

· · ·

I regarded the Village People's image asexually. It never occurred to me that the Construction Worker on the cover of *Cruisin'*, sprawled atop a digger truck, his shirt unbuttoned all the way down to his thrusted-out crotch, comported himself in that way for any other reason than to be more comfortable. Or that the Motorcycle Man wore black leather chaps for any other reason than protection from road burn riding his hog in the desert.

The Village People were having fun. They represented a cross section of society.

◆ ◆ ◆

A wise person once said that you don't have to justify the music you loved at 11 or 12.

That wise person was me. I just wrote that just now.

◆ ◆ ◆

I played trombone. I took up the instrument because my father played trombone, but also because I thought it was simple to master. I was wrong. The trombone is the Village People of musical instruments, built by committee, equal parts trumpet, piston flute, tuba, and phallic symbol. As a 10-year-old male trombonist, I pursed my lips on this monstrosity, moved the slide in and out, puberty's dress rehearsal for the boners and voice cracks.

◆ ◆ ◆

Four years I squirted lube up and down the trombone slide. Extended out to its furthest, seventh position, the trombone spanned the open area of my room, from the end of my bed where I sat to the music stand propped up in the corner. For months I focused on the B-flat major scale and the theme from *Rocky*— specifically two notes after the trumpet fanfare—which marked one of the rare times I got to play melody at OLPH's band recital.

◆ ◆ ◆

I used to say I had two first albums. For years, I claimed I bought *Cruisin'* the same day as Billy Joel's 1980 album, *Glass Houses*, that same afternoon at Peaches. This is just untrue: the records came out two years apart. Here, clearly, is another example of where I've tried to make myself look cooler to the outside world. Not that the album with "Still Rock and Roll to Me" should get me off the hook entirely. The truth is, I played trombone along to the Village People's "My Roommate"—which was, as we say now, *my jam*—and improvised free jazz-type solos that drove my mother out of the house, even when I muted the bell with a plunger.

Notes on a Sad, Pitiful
Baseball Career

From space, Maple Shade's borders resemble a baby elephant in profile. Or maybe a rhinoceros's head. Looking at Google Earth today, I had forgotten how the town extends across Route 38, along the interstate, a gerrymander that bulwarks the apartment complexes neither Cherry Hill nor Moorestown wanted on its school rolls.

I like to zoom in over our old house. The new owners have set up an aboveground pool and a white privacy fence. I can see the slow decline of the hill, the dark-green crabgrass.

. . .

Beyond our block and around the curve of our street sits a black circle. This is Maple Shade's sewage processing plant. At street level, all we saw was a mysterious carousel arm that sprayed liquid over what looked to be wet, black coals. The boys in town nicknamed this *aeration ring,* as the township website calls it, the "Shitty-Go-Round." It only occurs to me years later, looking down from sky, that living next to the town's shitwater sieve probably kept our property values down.

. . .

Further east are what looks like several orange teardrops with green centers lining the back of West Woodlawn Avenue. These are the baseball and softball fields of Maple Shade. Right behind our house is the outfield of the biggest baseball field, complete with a clubhouse and PA speakers. If the field was a stadium, our backyard would sit in the 100 section, 20 rows back from right field. The only thing keeping home run balls from landing in our backyard was a 20-foot guard fence and a dirt path in right field. Farther down, next to the never-used-for-tennis tennis court, sat the CYO field. That's where I would play. Or, to be more accurate, that is where I would stand in the batter's box, strike out, then drown my sorrows in fountain sodas, Swedish fish, and soft pretzels.

• • •

Springtime in The Shade revolved around boys' baseball. Orange clay and line chalk blew behind our house in the mornings, as volunteers got the fields ready for a full day of games. As a kid, I'd lie in bed as a succession of scratchy Star-Spangled Banners played from the clubhouse PAs. Sunlight peeked through drawn drapes. Old men announced lineups in flat monotone: *Next batter, for the Dodgers, Stephen Kassakert. Next batter, for the Cardinals, Tommy Babcock.*

• • •

Walking and biking around the streets of Maple Shade, I'd wonder why I was such an easy mark for ridicule. I wasn't any more gawky or nerdy than many other kids. Socially, I was awkward, taller than most. Who among us wasn't an awkward prepubescent? We've gone over the trombone-playing business. I also didn't excel at sports or acts of random violence boys liked at that developmental stage, but these shortcomings alone shouldn't have been enough to make me a target. The only answer I can come up with is baseball, and how badly I sucked at it.

From 1976 to 1982, I was the worst player in Maple Shade's Catholic Youth Organization. No one came close. I might've been the worst ever. We could play this up for laughs, but please know that when I cite my lifetime batting average of .057 playing right field, and how I never got more than one base hit each season, we are talking about a formative humiliation that cuts deep to the present day.

• • •

To compensate for being Maple Shade's strikeout king, I developed an ironic distance. I acted like I didn't care and at the same time expected to be selected for the all-star team each year. This, I can see now, only led to more ridicule. Somewhere along the line, I just thought I was somehow *better than that*, or felt more deserving of praise than I really was. I felt entitled to be a cool kid when I should have been content to sit at the Retarded Kids Table with the other kids in the A-Level Reading Group, or the boys with stunted growth who cowered in the corner, or the one or two boys who turned out to be genuinely gay.

• • •

The only sure way to get on base, I figured, was to get hit by a pitch. When that happens, you get to go to first base. It's as good as a hit. The first time was a championship game in 1980, the Cardinals versus the A's. The bases were loaded with two outs, and we were losing by one run. Our third base coach, a player's dad who sipped from a flask he kept in his back pocket, shouted at me before I entered the left-hander's batter's box.

"Just put your bat on the ball!" He curled his hands around his mouth to make sure I heard him. "Just get the bat on the ball!"

The pitcher threw so hard the ball hissed toward the plate. I couldn't even see the ball. My undiagnosed myopia turned out to be a good thing. If had seen it, I would've ducked or dove or run away. So I turned my right ass cheek toward the pitcher over home plate, and *swack!*

Everything goes quiet at the field when a ball hits a small boy. But I was overjoyed. After the look-over by ump, I flung the bat toward the dugout and jogged to first base. Good as a hit. Tie game.

◆ ◆ ◆

For my last two years playing baseball, I led the league in hit-by-pitches, with at least 10 per season. If the pitcher didn't throw a ball close enough for me to snag it with my butt, I bunted, a strategy that flabbergasted opposing teams. There I'd be, top of the third inning and no one on base, no call for a sacrifice or squeeze play, stooped over home plate with my bat out, well before the pitcher even began his wind-up.

"Danny Nester, the Bunt King," our coach, Mr. Kesari, called me.

◆ ◆ ◆

I still imagine what it would be like if I got, say, one hit a game, batted .250. Maybe I would have made more friends? Gotten in fewer fights? If I were better at baseball back then, I'd be a completely different person. I honestly believe that.

◆ ◆ ◆

In the off-season, older boys played pickup games and smacked home runs over the guard fence, which left dents in our aluminum siding. Some considerate outfielders screamed *Look-out!* as the ball sailed over, but most of the time there was a plink or crack of the bat, silence, and then a *thud* on the ground next to me as I mowed the lawn. Or a maybe a *ker-ploosh* into our tiny, aboveground pool. As a young boy, it seemed like an asteroid had hit the Earth, and the players who came to retrieve them were muscular, mustached spacemen.

· · ·

When we sold the house in 1987, we gave away the edger, sleds, end tables, and sets of tools. Anything that couldn't fit into Mom's apartment went into an uncle's pickup. It was August; the air was filled with the Shitty-Go-Round's humid sludge. I was assigned to clear out the garage. Last check around, the moving truck idling outside, and I looked up.

There, suspended from the rafters, was one of Dad's Navy duffle bags. It looked empty, but at the bottom of the camo canvas sack were about 30 scuffed-up baseballs and softballs.

Turns out Mike Nester had a policy to keep every home run ball that landed in his yard. He never threw them back; he just put them in the bag and sat back down in his lawn chair. I'd like to think it was his way of getting even, setting the cosmos right, moving just a couple beads on the heavenly abacus in the Nesters's favor.

11.

Notes on Reading

"There will come a day," Dad said, standing in the doorway of my room, "when you will wake up in the morning and have a Tremendous Quest for Knowledge." It will be a bold, bodily change, he assured me, and puffed out his chest and clenched his fists.

◆ ◆ ◆

Not so much a reader as a browser, I went for ready-reference digests over actually, you know, reading whole books. The Maple Shade Library was fine, but I preferred to build my own reference section, to collect and own knowledge. The Acme in town sold Funk and Wagnalls volumes of its wildlife encyclopedia, which I collected, along with pulpy titles from Scholastic Arrow Book Club, like *TV Time '78* and inspirational biographies of Babe Ruth or Lou Ferrigno. The stories I really loved involved people in costumes: *Mork and Mindy*, Buck Rogers, *Battlestar Galactica*, *The Dukes of Hazzard*, the Bee Gees. If the cover had person on it with sparkles affixed to their clothes, I needed that book.

◆ ◆ ◆

"I have been nourished on letters since my childhood," I underlined in my father's copy of *The Portable Descartes*. "I found myself embarrassed with so many doubts and errors that it seemed to me that the effort to instruct myself had no effect other than the increasing discovery of my own ignorance."

. . .

Dad bought me 3x5 cards, a metal case, and pens so I could write reviews of all the books I read. I filed each alphabetically by author.

. . .

Flesch, Rudolf

THE ART OF CLEAR THINKING

Excellent and concise guide to improving your wave of thought, think quicker and clearer, and think in a more organized way. Complete in every detail, with each chapter chock full of advice to help you solve a big problem. Interesting to read and has many tests and note taking tips. p. 196–197—tips on shorthand for often used words.

. . .

George Orwell

ANIMAL FARM

Brilliant and wittingly [sic] written satire on the system of Totalitarianism. It has [sic] the struggle between the animals and the incompetent farmer. Later the struggle shifts between all of the animals. Line for line throughout the story it paralels [sic] directly to dictatorships and communism.

At the beginning of the summer between sixth and seventh grade, he placed a stack of books on my dresser. "These are the books that will change your life," he said. The stack consisted of the following:

The Pilgrim's Progress by John Bunyan

The History of Western Civilization by Will Durant

Siddhartha by Hermann Hesse

The Book of Mormon

The True Believer by Eric Hoffer

The Koran

The Republic by Plato

The Autobiography of Benjamin Franklin

. . .

To prepare for the Tremendous Quest, I'd lie in my bed, covered with pamphlets and magazines, and stare at the ceiling. I rolled my hands over my ribs and waited for some physical transformation to begin.

12.

Notes on My Mother
(In Commandment Form)

I. I am your MOTHER, who gave birth to you. I am the big person, and you, my Child, are the pipsqueak.

II. Thou shalt spend a significant amount of your life waiting for your MOTHER, who will never leave the house without makeup.

III. Thou shall run and buy your MOTHER cigarettes at the M and C Deli whenever she needs a pack of Marlboro Reds (never a soft pack). To complete this task, your MOTHER shall provide a handwritten note granting permission for the purchase of said Marlboros (never a soft pack).

IV. Thou shalt learn to dodge the 12-foot curly phone cord your MOTHER whips across the kitchen, handset tucked in right shoulder.

V. Thou shalt not leave your bed unmade, the lawn unmowed, or dishes in the sink.

VI. Thou shalt not present your MOTHER business schemes, sleepover plans, or requests for special clothes; if you must, you may do so only when the vacuum cleaner is shut off.

VII. Your MOTHER reserves the right to express skepticism by raising her eyebrows above the rim of her glasses upon hearing your loopy business scheme, social plans for a sleepover supervised only by some shady divorced dad who lives out of town, or plan to buy the newest Members Only jacket.

VIII. Your MOTHER also reserves the right to express skepticism by repeating back the last words someone has said as individual, one-word questions.

Example:

```
MY SISTER:
Mom! Melissa invited me over
for a sleepover at her dad's
house in the Poconos.

MY MOM:
Sleep? Over? Poconos?
```

And when you hear your MOTHER's voice and thunderings you will remove yourself and stand afar.

IX. It is by turning statements into questions by your MOTHER that you will be made to then reconsider or recant your previous statement.

X. Thou shalt keep the Sabbath holy by keeping the volume on the television down.

．．．

My students over the years have been treated to my imitation of Patti, whenever I pretend to express naïve shock at what seems self-evident: "Rosie O'Donnell is a *lesbian*? Where did you hear *that*?" I do this to humanize myself, to tell them that, though I try hard to be a serious-minded, on-task pedagogue, there's always this voice, one that sounds like a cross of one of Marge Simpson's sisters and late-era Judy Garland, that may interject at any time to deflate a student's overblown sense of importance or questions about obvious things.

．．．

For reasons that will become obvious, I didn't talk to my father for this book. But I did talk to my mother for hours and hours, to help with family history and keep in check any over-dramatizations my child mind has added to my memories over the years. There's much about my relationship with her first husband that she didn't understand at the time. Patti focuses on silver linings, no matter how bad the circumstances. But when I asked her direct questions about substantial topics, she didn't bullshit me. Over the past 20 years, we have had quarrels and disagreements, particularly during the time she was married to her second husband, an ex-football player and erratic man with whom I rarely got along. It's really only in the past ten years, after her second husband died suddenly and I married and became a father, that we have reached another part of our relationship where we speak frankly to each other, more like two mature adults than mother and son. She hadn't thought about some of this stuff for years. My point being: she had no axe to grind. I have no reason to think she's embellishing or has scores to settle, and while talking to her, she's been as much of a collaborator as a source.

13.

Notes on *The Good Bad Boy*

I knew three things about Mark Little, my mother's younger brother:

1. He was a total badass, a New Jersey State Trooper our family nicknamed "Bear";

2. He was my godfather, and in that capacity was permitted to crush my hand like a soft-shell crab when he greeted me at family get-togethers; and

3. He was no longer a Roman Catholic.

· · ·

Item #3 stuck out most. Mark's ex-Catholic status was mentioned but never explained. Other than Dad's agnosticism, no one in the family led a life outside the church. Uncle Mark, defender of the Garden State Parkway's speed limit, possessor of pistol and shotgun, source of my grandfather's pride, owner of a house in the Jersey Pines, pulled over my aunts' boyfriends on Forklanding Road as they drove off from dates, firing up the siren on his civilian vehicle, patting them down, and letting them go. Weeks later, the suitor would see Mark sitting in my grandmother's kitchen.

· · ·

While Mark and the other men in my family watched Iggles games, I rummaged through my grandparents' attic. Beside a stash of *National Geographics* and JC Penney catalogues, I'd lean against my aunt's hope chest and stare at naked bush women and women in bras, and enter a state of erotic wonder that I would now call Not Yet Masturbating.

One day, I dug up an old hardbound book with a gold-embossed cover and deckle-edged sides. Inscribed on the inside cover in a boy's hand: "The book belongs to Mark Little, 1961." Published by The Neumann Press in 1949, Father Gerald Brennan's *The Good Bad Boy: The Diary of an Eighth-Grade Boy* tells the story of Pompey Briggs as he enters eighth grade at Holy Cross School.

"Great men always keep diaries," Briggs writes. "Perhaps, that's what makes them great. If I keep a diary, I, too, may become great. Who knows?"

• • •

The book had me at its oxymoronic title. How can a bad boy be good, or a good boy bad? I didn't know which of these boys I wanted to be, though I leaned toward being the bad one who could be good when he wanted to. *The Good Bad Boy* was written by a priest—a pastor of Our Lady of Mount Carmel Parish in Rochester, New York—which gave the book Catholic street cred. To say I related to Pompey understates things. For the months I read and reread it, I *was* the Good Bad Boy.

• • •

The Good Bad Boy appeared around the same time I was barred from ordering *The Catcher in the Rye* from the Scholastic Books catalog. One of the nuns told me it was "too adult," that I "wasn't ready for it yet," which made me want to read the book more. Pompey Briggs was a good enough stand-in for Holden Caulfield. In *Love and Death in the American Novel*, Leslie Fiedler defines the Good Bad Boy as "America's vision of itself, crude and unruly in his beginnings, but endowed by his creator with an instinctive sense of what is right. Sexually as pure as any milky maiden, he is a roughneck all the same, at once potent and submissive, made to be reformed by the right woman." American fiction's "fear of sex, a strange blindness to the daily manifestations of sex, or the attenuation of sexuality itself drove the American novel back over the lintel of puberty in the declining years of the nineteenth century." Huck Finn, watered down into Beaver Cleaver and Dennis the Menace later on, grew more false in their naïveté, hostile to teachers and culture, as opposed to the pure skepticism of the Good Bad Boy.

I envisioned myself as a scamp but not a reprobate, an antihero willing to be converted if the cause was just and the time was right.

◆ ◆ ◆

I always wondered why my Uncle Mark left the church. Was it as simple as marrying my Aunt Jodi, a Protestant? The real reason, he told me at a family party after several Coors Lites, was that he felt guilty all the time as a Catholic boy.

"I'd play with myself and run right to church to go to confession," he said. He did this every day. "Even the priest told me I shouldn't be so hard on myself." When Mark met my Aunt Jodi right out of the trooper academy, and left the house, he just stopped going to church. His story, once I heard it, did not seem strange to me.

◆ ◆ ◆

Pompey Briggs inspired me to keep my own journal, as I insisted on calling it—not a "diary," which I regarded as girly and insubstantial. I wrote out entries on an Acme paper pad and put the completed sheets back into a cigar box.

"You must be prepared for the Test of Life," I wrote in my first entry on December 21, 1981. "Are you making Progress? Or are you falling into the bottomless pit of Failure, an infinite void where so many of us have forced us [sic] to fall into?"

Each night I curled my biceps into meatball-shaped masses, sat on my knees and prayed against the bed, and, with muscles throbbing, wrote promises to myself. From another early entry: "I shall be a scholar and write a monumental work to be praised hundreds of years to come."

It's hard to reconcile this boy with the one who cupped his hands to make fart noises in class. The man can't go back and tell the boy to lighten up, scale down his dreams a bit. Still, I can't help but root for this potent and submissive kid who yearned to write monumental works.

Notes on the Little Family

There's a joke, a parable really, often repeated by members of my family, that explains our clan's approach to life. I think it's adapted from an old Danny Thomas routine. It's called "The Farmer's Jack."

• • •

It goes like this. One rainy night, a man is driving down a country road when he gets a flat tire. He pulls over and opens his trunk to look for his spare and tire jack. But the jack is missing. There's not another car in sight. What can he do now?[6]

He decides to walk to the nearest house and borrow a jack. Down the road, over some hills, he sees the lights of a farmhouse. "Farmers are helpful people," he says. "I'll borrow the farmer's jack."

He starts the long walk. The rain comes down harder. The man steps in puddles and his shoes are wet. He says, "As long as he's awake, this will be worth the effort."

Then he has to climb over a barbed wire fence to cross a field, and he cuts his hands. "The farmer is sleeping," he says. "What if I wake him up and he's in a bad mood? What if he doesn't have a jack in the first place?"

---

6 This story predates the age of the cell phone, obviously. And suburban sprawl.

He slips in the field. Mud is all over his pants and his shirt. Now he's getting frustrated. "What if the farmer isn't friendly? What if he charges money for the jack?"

As he approaches the farmhouse, he steps in cow dung. By now the man is cold and covered in mud; he smells like shit, and he's just plain angry. "I bet he's asleep, he'll be rude, and he'll give me a hard time about borrowing his jack," he says. "I'll just get this over with."

He walks up to the farmhouse and pounds on the door. He sees the lights go on, and a couple minutes later the farmer comes downstairs in his pajamas. Just when the farmer is about to open the door, the man shouts, "Ah, forget about it—shove the jack up your ass!"

And the man walks away.

◆ ◆ ◆

In our family, we expect things to go wrong. Our distorted thinking has led us to convince ourselves we don't deserve anything. We called it our "shove-the-jack-up-your-ass" mindset.

"Always expect the worst," my grandparents would say. "That way, if things don't turn out that way, you'll be pleasantly surprised."

◆ ◆ ◆

Daniel Curtis Little, my mother's father and my namesake, grabbed headlines as Frankford High's soccer star. He led the team when they won the 1926 Philadelphia Public League Finals. At 20, Curt, as he was called, met 16-year-old Helen Fontaigne through a fellow Eagle Scout who was dating her "Jewish best friend," Rita Scheinoff. Helen said she was "simple" back then, by which she meant nerdy, funny, giggly.

On their first date, Curt showed up at Helen's front door up in full Eagle Scout uniform. This horrified Helen. Technically, he wasn't even a full Eagle Scout, the story goes, since he refused to lie, as his fellow scouts did, and claim he had spotted a yellow-bellied sapsucker to get his final badge.

"Your Grandpop was too honest, even for the Eagle Scouts," Mom would say.

• ◆ •

They wed in 1940. After the bombing of Pearl Harbor, Curt went straight into the Navy as a pipefitter aboard the U.S.S. *Crescent City*. He sent Helen epic love letters from the Pacific, enough to fill two shoeboxes. They used code words for battles at Guadalcanal, Bougainville, and Guam. As the final Japan assault approached, Curt composed three farewell letters, for three different scenarios: air attack, beach invasion, or sunk at sea. No one on his ship thought they would survive. Then the atomic bombs fell on Hiroshima and Nagasaki. Helen and Curt reunited in Philadelphia. If it weren't for those mushroom clouds, everyone except Grandpop said, we wouldn't be here.

• ◆ •

They moved to Maple Shade in 1950. In another age and town, and if she were a man, Helen Little could have been a mover-and-shaker in politics. She settled for working as an assistant to the township manager and chairing the Maple Shade Democratic Club. She kept a CB radio at her desk; her handle was "Municipal Mama." My mother remembers how Helen raked Curt over the coals, said he "never earned a good living." I remember Curt differently. He worked hard at manual jobs for 30 years, in factories and mills, with a stint as a milkman somewhere as well. The work was often dangerous. At one work site, he welded in foot-deep water without protective gear. Eventually, the boss closed shop when union men approached his crew. Curt rounded out his career at a print shop that made exit-by-exit punch cards used by the Turnpike Authority. After the shop went out of business, Curt lost his pension.

·　·　·

Curt Little's contribution to the English language was the word -*suck* used as a suffix. He stuck them after names of people he despised, mostly Republicans or baseball players.

He showed particular disdain for Phillies third baseman and future hall of famer Mike Schmidt. "Schmidtsuck, don't swing at every pitch!" he'd shout above announcer Harry Kalas.

Many a family meal's political discussion would reach a crescendo with invocations of *Nixon-suck*, *Frank Rizzo-suck*, or *Bush-suck*.

"I'll tell you something if you all just quiet down for a second," Curt said after the election of Ronald Reagan. "Can I tell you something? The only administration I got laid off was Eisenhower-suck's. And he was a Republican!"

·　·　·

I remember my grandparents in their 50s, still full of piss and vinegar. Grandpop lorded over me, anticipating my every move. If I even thought of touching something I shouldn't touch—his car door locks, his sister Esther's couch cushions, his brother Buddy's chintzy lamps—there he'd appear, a Spectral Teller of Cautionary Tales, shout-whispering over my shoulder.

"Keep your hands off that gizmo," he'd say. "What are you, an animal?"

Helen indulged her grandson's melodrama, which she met with ultimate seriousness. She poured orange juice through a strainer to take out the pulp—I thought they were *little fishies* and feared they would live inside my stomach forever. I shared my tales of woe, and she cheered me up with cookies and canned pineapple chunks.

My grandparents embodied the Irish-German, Catholic, no-nonsense, stop-crying, Shader approach to life, the sum of all Phillies and A's seasons, the wooden and plastic seats of Connie Mack and Vet Stadiums, the side tables with Schmitz beer and pretzels next to recliners. And telling the farmers of the world to shove their jacks up their asses.

15.

Notes on the Mega Test

The Summer of Love arrived at our house on West Woodlawn Avenue a full two decades after 1967. My mom read Leo Buscaglia pop psychology books, while Dad listened to whale call cassettes and ordered vitamin supplements and home wine-making kits from ads in the back of *Mother Earth News*. We traced biorhythm charts with a Spirograph-looking instrument that determined if our energies were compatible, if we were having "up" or "down" days. Mom and Dad were hippies after the rest of the world had moved on. And then came the IQ tests.

• • •

The "Mega Test" was published in a 1985 issue of *Omni*. Published by *Penthouse's* Bob Guccione's son, *Omni* mixed science fiction and other nerd-friendly fare. "There have been various tests devised over the years that make fine distinctions in the intellectual stratosphere," the article reads. "The idea is to make a test so difficult that geniuses will get average scores, and only super-geniuses will be able to achieve the highest scores." The questions try to stump the super-smart with spatial and numerical problems and analogies such as:

BLACK : YELLOW :: MELANCHOLIC : ?

PAIN : RUE :: BREAD : ?

One rainy day, Dad cleared off the kitchen table and we all took the test. I did well—8 right for an IQ of 134. I was smart, but not a "Mega Genius." My father's score was through the roof—22 correct for an IQ of 150. A few weeks later, he passed the test for Mensa, a society for people with high IQs. He made plans to attend his first meeting of the Delaware Valley Mensa's Philosophy Group. The topic of discussion: *Zen and the Art of Motorcycle Maintenance.*

Dad had already read Robert Pirsig's best-selling book, a philosophical novel-essay about "the fabulous journey of a man in search of himself." Framed around a father-son motorcycle journey from St. Paul to San Francisco, *Motorcycle Maintenance* seemed like the perfect book for us to bond over. We could talk about repairing motorcycles as a Zen activity, or have a Chautauqua, which I took to mean a long conversation about intellectual things. I scanned through the second half of the book the night of his meeting, understanding little, to prepare for our own discussion the next morning. Here's my index card review:

Pirsig, Robert M.
ZEN AND THE ART OF MOTORCYCLE MAINTENANCE
A mysterious trip through the mind of the author takes us from deep, philosophical thoughts to the weak plot desperately trying to keep throughout the story. covers many things such as classical and romantic thought and how these collide as well as blend. what the book is in reality [is an] an essay or treatise on anything under the sun. The book is for me at this time very hard to read, but I believe I have received the general messages of the story.

. . .

Over breakfast, I asked Dad about the Mensa meeting.

"I left early," he said. "It was just a bunch of people bullshitting."

He hated how they talked, he explained, how each prefaced his or her remarks with "basically," which he imitated in a drawn-out moan: *Baaaaa-sically*.

. . .

The Delaware Valley Mensans spoke in *baaaaa-sically* the same way academics do now, except they end statements like questions and say "problematize" a lot. I imagine Dad coming back from the dead and traveling through time to attend a conference with me, how his skin would crawl, or how he'd just walk out.

Notes on Money, Sweat, and Jesus

We never had money, and when we did we spent it on stupid name-brand stuff, because that's what people with no money do with money once they get it. If we found a five-dollar bill, the first impulse wasn't to sock it away. It was to get in the car and buy junk food at full price at the Wawa, or go to the mall to get Sergio Valentes for Meri. When we did catch up with bills, Dad would do something really stupid, like put a down payment on a new pickup truck.

Broke people with money buy ostentatious things. They parade those things around in front of still-broke people. I didn't notice we were broke—or, as Mom put it, *bad with money*—until I heard other Shaders bragging about their fancy sneakers or designer jeans, things we didn't have.

· · ·

Mom handled the bills. It was her job to take calls from collectors. Dad never wanted to hear it. I heard them argue from my room.

"What do you want me to do, Patti?" Dad shouted. "Squat and *shit* money?"

· · ·

I complained about money. I wanted quarters for the arcade, to get sneakers or candy.

"So get a job," they said.

I got my first job in fifth grade, working for Vince Penza, beloved parish janitor and general groundskeeper at Our Lady of Perpetual Help. We vacuumed classrooms, swept between pews, and repainted classrooms in the summer. To join the ranks of "Vince's Boys" was considered an honor. We were like little monks with mops.

．　．　．

At five foot three, Vince wore dress pants and short-sleeved shirts with a pocket protector. Sets of keys drooped from his belt. As he genuflected past the church crucifix, Vince sounded like a human sleigh bell. He whistled Frank Sinatra and Johnny Mathis tunes outdoors. I became an expert in calculating Vince's location as the sound of his whistle and key-jingles bounced between the rectory and school.

It took me months to figure out what Vince was saying. What kind of speech impediment he had I cannot say. "Nessen, go ousside and clean the dirby windles," he'd say. My name would always be Nessen, and I would clean the dirby windles.

"Puke is clean when it first comes out, Nessen," Vince assured me as I cleaned up a first-grader's mess. "Just mop it up and drain the bucket."

．　．　．

On the Feast of the Annunciation, Vince taught me how to fix a hole in the wall. I sat all day with a hawk and trowel and scooped plaster into a hole in the shape of some doofus fourth-grader's head. Working in an overheated school with all the windows closed got me sweating like a pig. I took my shirt off and heard Vince's whistling down the hallway.

"Nessen! Whaddya doin' with your shirt off? You can't work without a shirt!" Vince tugged at the tank top tucked in my jeans. "The nuns might see you!"

I put my shirt back on. Vince gave me an unsolicited piece of advice: there's nothing embarrassing about a grown man shaving his armpits. Since then, whenever I swipe my pits with a razor, I think of Vince Penza.

· · ·

The pay was $1.50 an hour, under the table, in cash. Vince added up hours in shaky handwriting on the back of church envelopes. Once I started getting money, I decided I didn't want leather high-tops or designer jeans. I wanted a moped. The cheapest street-legal scooters cost $400, a fortune for my parents. So I started my own Moped Fund. As I write this, I'm looking at two Columbia Savings Bank passbooks with deposits of $15, made every Friday afternoon.

· · ·

Working at my church felt like I was part of some divine movie crew, a key grip who rang bells for morning mass, replaced candles, and sent vestments to a sacred laundry service. My faith deepened. I attended mass two or three times a week. I became, for lack of a better term, a Jesus freak. I considered joining the priesthood or becoming a deacon. But my body had other plans.

17.

Notes on My Sister, the Fox

Around Maple Shade, people still refer to me as "Meri Nester's brother." Meredith Ann Nester's look perfectly suited the early-1980s: long, blonde hair (enhanced by Sun-In), Bongo jeans from Merry-Go-Round, cut sweat shirts, and jelly pumps. I wore husky Wranglers, tube socks, and glasses that remained tinted indoors. Meri made varsity cheerleading by eighth grade. I played trombone and sent away for free pamphlets from the Consumer Information Catalog. Meri was the barefoot girl in Bruce Springsteen's "Jungleland" who sat on the hood of a Dodge and drank warm beer in the soft summer rain. I'm the misfit who listened to Rush's "Subdivisions," and wondered how a Canadian band knew that the suburbs had no charms to soothe the restless dreams of my youth.

If Meri Nester reacted to Maple Shade like I did, I might not have gone crazy. But she didn't react to Maple Shade like I did. And so I did go crazy.

• • •

Meri took things in stride. Meri took The Shade in stride. Meri wanted to experience this thing called *fun*. She wanted to engage in this activity called *hanging out* and surrounded herself with an entourage of like-minded Shader foxes I'd otherwise never meet. They all *hung out* and had *fun*.

"Oh, you're Meri Nester's *older brother*?" Shader dudes said to me on the baseball field. "I didn't know she had a *brother*." Pause. "Your sister's a *fox*."

What went unsaid was *Geez, your sister is pretty and fun, and you're the guy who sits in front of the Wawa and reads* Mad *magazine.*

• • •

When my friends in band started calling Meri a fox to my face, I realized I was regarded as the Hunchback of West Woodlawn Avenue, who was hidden away for fear of bringing shame upon our family. I was a feral dork best kept indoors.

• • •

The fox, the Greek poet once wrote, *knows many things.* It resists boiling the world down to one idea. That was Meri. She knew everyone in town and was friends with all of them. I was a *hedgehog* which the same poet observed *obsesses over one big thing,* which was why I didn't fit in.

• • •

Meri outwitted me at every turn. She was the Bugs Bunny to my Yosemite Sam, the Ferris Bueller to my Jeanie Bueller. She had better grades, scored higher on tests, and was more evenly tempered than her dramatic older brother. As she moved gracefully among Maple Shade's social sets, boys jammed sticks in my bike spokes, which sent the trombone case propped on my handlebars forward like a projectile, followed by my large, hedgehog head.

• • •

At home, Meri rearranged my carefully alphabetized cassette wall shelf just to fuck with me. If I gave her any guff, she pulled my hands toward her chest, a working-the-ref tactic she knew would bring out the warrior-protector in Mom.

"Don't touch her there!" she shouted. "Don't you know her body is going through *changes*?"

• • •

Meri wasn't embarrassed *by me*; she was embarrassed *for me*. I would walk down the street by myself, a boombox on my shoulder playing a mix of the latest soft rock, and there would be my sister with a flight of friends engaged in suburban sacraments, their purses stuffed with pony bottles of beer some old man scored for them.

Meri broke away from her group to say hello, but it was more out of pity than a genuine happiness to see me. We both knew what was going on. Our town quickly sorts out the gawky from the graceful.

18.

Notes on Mike Nester's Second Jobs and Get-Rich-Quick Schemes: A Timeline

1967: Prompted by reading an article on prices of fur in local newspaper, plans to run a chinchilla farm out of one-bedroom apartment in Ocean View, Virginia. Buys supplies; farm never gets off ground.

1968–1969: Sells large photo albums with padded covers and baby furniture door-to-door in Virginia Beach area.

1972: Sells vending machines; training consists of memorizing sales spiel, the main component of which is to "symbolically break bread" with prospective customer—in this case a sample of cookies and crackers from said vending machine.

If the customer is not willing to break cracker or cookie, the training materials asserted, you could pretty well assume the sale was in the dumpster.

1974: Sells round, concrete pool tables intended for outdoor use at resort areas with school friend, Bob "Beaver" McFarland. Two other friends, Freddie and Jimmie, also get in on surefire plan.

"It was Beaver's spiel this time," Mom explains. Beaver and crew are assigned the Wildwood, New Jersey, area. A single, concrete pool table reportedly still blights Wildwood's boardwalkscape.

1976: Inspired by man who sold dollar cans of beer at the Bicentennial Beach Boys concert on the steps of the Philly Art

Museum, he decides that he, too, will sell beer at successive concerts for the same substantial mark-up. The next week, he arrives with two cases on ice in his Navy duffel bag, wearing overalls and no shirt. This concert, however, is not a rock concert; it is a quiet, opera music event, sparsely attended. At the first shout of "Cold beer here!" he is stopped by a Philly cop, who tells him to stop and takes one of his Budweisers.

1977: Small investments in gold, soybean futures, supplementary life insurance.

1978: Attends Glassboro State College on the G.I. Bill with ambitions to become high school history teacher. Takes one course in Western Civilization. Lasts for half a semester. Receives a grade of "Incomplete."

1978: File cabinets overflow with new business plans. Og Mandino's *The Greatest Salesman in the World*. "Maximum human potential" tape sets.

1980: Flirtations with Herbalife, skin and health care products produced from aloe plants. Grows aloe plants in bay window, rubs cuttings on children's skin to test the substance's efficacy.

Notes on Amway

Patti listened patiently to each of Mike's Ponzi plans or found-in-the-back-of-a-magazine sales kits, skeptical but supportive.

"The mind was always working," Mom says out on the rear deck. There comes a point, in these discussions, where she goes outside her own house to smoke, which she does only when we visit with our girls. "I just didn't see why he couldn't just let things *be*."

• ♦ •

Mike Nester joined Amway in 1979—"prospected," in Amway-speak, by Aunt Chrissy and Uncle Tony, her first husband, who I will later hear worked as a small-time bookie and cocaine dealer. This occurred just months before it was deemed a pyramid scheme by the Federal Trade Commission and not a "multi-level marketing company." As an Independent Business Owner (IBO), Dad sold dry goods, like liquid organic soap and vitamins, but mostly tried to get others join the organization. To make any money at Amway, you need to bring at least 225 people into your fold.

• ♦ •

One Saturday, Dad set up a tape recorder in the living room to record his first Amway meeting. Amway's literature advises new IBOs to tape their early meetings for self-assessment purposes. He invited a few swing shift coworkers from Boss-Linco

Trucking to talk about the wonders of Amway. Mom brewed coffee, bought a sheet cake from the Acme, and filled the fridge with cans of Bud.

. . .

I helped Dad set up the tape recorder on the coffee table. "Amway meeting numero uno," Dad says on the tape. "Mic check, mic check..."

Chrissy and Tony played the role of assistants. To demonstrate Amway's drain cleaner, they put dirt inside of a Styrofoam cup and poured in soap. It was like watching a Doug Henning magic special. On the tape, you hear the drain cleaner sizzle through the dirt, the *oohs* and *aahs* of Dad's coworkers, and then a *thud!* as soap-and-dirt goo lands on the coffee table. It left a permanent stain my mother would complain about for years to come.

. . .

I buzzed around the room that Saturday, revved up on sugar, as a roomful of truckers with names like Dee-Pee (for "Displaced Person"), Joey "It's In My Pants" Pancressi, and Lippy, an African American with large lips, flipped through company pamphlets and drank cans of beer. They all bought small bottles of Liquid Organic Concentrate (LOC) and passed on the prospecting.

That was it for Amway. Mom repurposed the blue plastic cart that held the starter kit as a gardening tote.

. . .

My Aunt Chrissy reminded me of the motivational posters that hung beside his desk, the pillow speaker he bought to fall asleep to Amway tapes, the glossy photos of televangelist-looking men in plaid suits, "Diamond Direct Distributors" with magnificent hair and deep tans, their wives with lockjawed smiles posing in

high-ceilinged rooms. Dad came back from Amway meetings—
"pumped up like I'd never seen him," Mom says now—with plans
for a pilgrimage to Amway's Mecca: Ada, Michigan.

Notes on Shriek Alarms

I remember Dad's pitch for his last scheme: he had mysteriously come into possession of a box with a gross of "shriek alarms." The plan this time, he explained, was to sell them on consignment at checkout counters. Mom's response was not a surprise.

"Shriek? Alarms?"

Shriek alarms, Dad told her, are for women who are in empty parking lots and need to scare away rapists or attract help.

"Parking lots? Rapists?"

Dad took what looked like a metal toilet paper tube out of the box. I read the packaging. "Ten times louder than a human scream, these ear-piercing shriek alarms will disorientate attackers and will provide valuable seconds for you to get away!" He lifted it to the ceiling, pressed the top with index and middle finger, and out came a high-pitched sound, a shriek, *eeeeeeeeeeeeek!*—a soprano foghorn that sent our dog, Snuffy, howling at the moon.

• • •

Personal safety had remained an issue for me in The Shade, and having my own supply of shriek alarms seemed to offer a solution. Getting whaled by tennis balls in the OLPH schoolyard was one thing, but on the streets of Maple Shade, the Musgrove brothers had started a campaign of terror, this time with rocks. Born six months apart, each Musgrove resembled Sluggo Smith, with round, buzzed heads and fleshy boxer's noses. They walked around town like Ugandan death squads. Whenever they saw me, they'd wing a rock at my trombone case. Maybe, I thought, I can use a shriek alarm to disorientate them or cry for help.

Dad put the box in the cabin of his pickup truck and we drove around to do his pitch. We went to the Acme, the 5 & 10, Smith's Pharmacy, a couple of car washes, and the Maple Shade Bakery.

Local shopkeepers, oddly, were averse to having a display of rape alarms on their front counter, or at least ones sold to them on consignment from a hairy truck driver.

◆ ◆ ◆

Out of pity, the Pep Boys on Main Street allowed a few to be set beside the cash register. The rest were placed in a box in my corner area of the garage.

For the next three or four years, I had free rein over the shriek alarm surplus. I did get to sound one off on a Musgrove brother once. He just stood there, waiting for it to be over, then threw a handful of rocks at my sneakers.

21.

Notes on the Ceramic Apple, in the Third Person

He found an old photograph hidden inside a ceramic apple, kept on top of the family fridge. It pictures the Fourth of July parade in Maryville, Tennessee. The family was visiting relatives, his father's side. In the photo, he is 12 years old. He is wearing shorts, and his skinny legs are flung wide. The photographer, his mother, was standing across the street. In the photo, he refuses to smile.

•   •   •

Both of his hairless testicles can be seen hanging out. They are plainly visible.

•   •   •

Why did his mother hold on to this embarrassment? Why was it kept all those years inside a ceramic apple, tucked under tacks, spare batteries, orphaned birthday candles? Whole color guards passed his balls, flag-bearers and Volunteer State veterans stood in salute of his sagging family jewels.

That was the day he met Dicky Bird Nester, his cousin, who owned a speedboat. He told Dicky Bird about how he played trombone, how he knew the bass part to that famous Coke commercial, "I'd Like to Teach the World to Sing," in which children from different parts of the globe hold candles and smile for the camera.

22.

Notes on Puberty, also in the Third Person

He felt his body change. At first, he thought it was a tremor or a nervous tick or maybe heat stroke. Or maybe he was just excited about high school? Or maybe it was his Quest for Knowledge?

"I shall try to be a good and wholesome person, imitating Our Lord Jesus Christ and the brilliant thinker and philosopher Socrates," he wrote in his journal. "I must be satisfied with strictly internal, personal pleasure. Oh, how I am tempted to throw away all responsibility and turn to Satan."

• • •

He buzzes around his room, waxes the dresser, alphabet-izes cassettes, paints a red stripe across the wall with brush and tape—anything to avoid going to bed and deal with his body, his stupid humming body, the sinful body attached to his brain.

• • •

Things that feel dirty:

The girl at the custard stand who spread jimmies on his cone.

The Moorestown girls with bob haircuts who sunbathed by Strawbridge Lake.

Gloria, who lived by the train bridge, who *would do anything with anybody*, the boys said.

Leg warmers.

Girlie mags stashed under Little League benches.

Shader girls who strutted down Main Street.

Solid Gold Dancers, Pinky Tuscadero, Daphne Blake from Scooby-Doo, Cat Woman, Olivia Newton-John.

◆　◆　◆

But most of all, he had dirty thoughts about real girls, the girls who played clarinet and flute and sat in front of him, their butts bubbled out of folding chairs. Endless daydreams of tenderly humping them.

◆　◆　◆

In case you haven't figured it out, we've reached the puberty part of his story. Springtide. The awkward stage. His chicken nuggets had browned in the oven. His acorns had fallen from the trees. His manly fountain had turned on.

23.

Notes on
Actual Things Said by My Mother:
A Commonplace

"Have you ever been to the Sex Mall in Hammonton? It's a BJ's, Dick's, and Seaman's Furniture Store."

"I thought mongoose was a bird. It has the word 'goose' in it."

"You want to know your Aunt Katie's philosophy on gynecologists? 'It's none of their business.' She never slept with her underwear on, either. She was a dancer."

"I never took birth control pills—I couldn't. I was Catholic. But your father wasn't, so that's why he wore balloons. He hated them. And if it broke, we'd go through this whole month of hell. I'm glad I can't get pregnant anymore."

"Two of my friends took birth control pills. They could also afford diaper service."

"My one sexual fantasy: An American Indian. He's a big strong man, like in *The Last of the Mohicans*, and he drags me into a nice, warm teepee with all sorts of furry things. And the light from the fire makes you look good."

"I hate Jeff Bridges. His tongue is too short for his mouth."

"When you get older, you get the puppet mouth. You look like Howdy Doody with your mouth going up and down."

"Grandmom didn't tell me anything—I learned everything from Bonnie Gilford, one of the class whores. Then I finally found out what 'it' was, where 'it' got placed."

"Terry and Chrissy remember me sitting them down on a couch and saying, 'What I'm going to tell you is probably the grossest thing you'll ever hear.' I got this pop-up book with these animals—horses, pigs, cows, all having sex. A bunny on top of another bunny. When it got to the humans, all it showed was a dad turning the light off, and the mother covered in a blanket. When Terry had her class on the birds and the bees, Mary Auld and I took her book and went into the bathroom with mirrors to see what all the parts they were talking about. We didn't know some of them."

"I thought you got pregnant from being too close to someone—not leaving enough room for the Holy Spirit."

"The rich girls from Merchantville didn't wear makeup and had sex with their boyfriends, and the Catholic girls from Maple Shade wore gobs of makeup and were virgins until their wedding night."

"Mike tried to convince all of us that turkeys were mammals and bore live young. They even breastfed the kids. He called them 'turkey pups.' "

"My mom wouldn't tell me what a box she had called Just Because was. Turns out it was a brand of tampon."

"It was almost a date rape. I thought were going to the Cherry Hill Inn—a really posh place—but here it was at Woodlyn Fire Hall. I wore a black crêpe dress, a flower embedded in it. I was over-dressed for this firehouse wedding. He was a great-looking guy, from a big Irish family in Glendora, a brother of a girl I worked with. And he goes to drive me home—but parks at Cooper River. It was on the other side of the lake, where I'm not used to parking. And his hands were all over me in seconds. I fended him off, and he took me back home. That's why I always say it's good for ladies to keep their nails long and with a good coat of polish on them."

"I used to think men's testicles were attached to their legs. I wondered how gymnasts did what they did, with their testicles attached to their upper thighs."

"I always get Battleship Potemkin and Mandy Patinkin mixed up."

24.

Notes on Shaders

Shaders have a saying: "You can take a Shader out of The Shade, but you can't take The Shade out of a Shader."

. . .

Shaders heard the town siren in the middle of town whenever there was a big fire. They got the afternoon *Bulletin*. Shaders were no-nonsense, happy, and helpful.

. . .

My parents' hands shook in 1971 when they signed the $17,000 mortgage for our rancher on West Woodlawn Avenue. It had a small addition for a third bedroom and recreation room. Its walls were covered in faux wood paneling. The old owners dug out a windowless basement for a boiler and water heater. My parents would soon know everyone by name, 20, 30 houses in each direction. When I was four, there was a fire in the house next door. The entire town came out to watch firemen hose down the roof. Someone came to sell soft pretzels out of an Acme shopping cart.

. . .

Shaders recall the Shady Maple Deli, Ronnie's Deli, Jim's Deli, M & C Deli, Cardella's, Big Daddy's Water Ice, the Maple Inn, Mike's Hardware, Buono's Market, Caruso's, Little Joe's Pizza, Angelo's Cold Cuts, the Red Carpet Lounge, the Apparel Shop (its slogan BEATSTHEMALL), and the China Star restaurant, which became a Hooters. Shaders pine for Harry's Cleaners, Ernesto's, the Benash Liquor sign. They miss Madge and Marge with their beehive hairdos, who lorded over kids as they walked the aisles of the 5 & 10, to make sure they didn't steal the shiny pinwheels, punch balloons, and Pixy Stix.

. . .

Shaders drove by the guy on Maple Avenue who wore a diaper as he worked on his garden, the people on Center Avenue with a monkey cage in their front lawn, the house that looked like a decommissioned Pizza Hut on South Forklanding Road.

. . .

Shader kids threw toilet paper and shaving cream on their neighbor's houses on Mischief Night. Shader boys played baseball and drank beer in the patch of woods near Pennsauken Creek (pronounced *crick*). Shader girls joined cheerleading or played field hockey and drank beer in the patch of woods near Pennsauken Creek.

Each time I came anywhere near Pennsauken Creek, someone pushed me into it, or I fell, and I walked home covered in mud, looking like something out of a Creature Double Feature.

. . .

Shader dads worked as bricklayers, varnish cooks, jig and die makers, Bell telephone installers, shipbuilders, diamond setters, bus mechanics, public service linemen, stereotypers, engineers, credit managers, soda salesmen, plumbers, hair stylists, bus drivers.

· · ·

Shaders held a sidewalk sale each September, ferried one another from the Happy Hour Club and The Jug Handle Inn, and got
into fights at the Jaycee Carnival beer garden each summer.

· · ·

There is no "Notable people" list in the Wikipedia entry for
Maple Shade Township, New Jersey; if there was such a section,
however, it would include Paul Baloche, a Christian singer-song-
writer who lives in Texas; John Tartaglia, a puppeteer who worked
as an understudy for Elmo at *Sesame Street* and co-created the
Tony Award-winning Broadway musical *Avenue Q;* an assortment
of retired Philadelphia Eagles such as Dick Bielski, Bob Pellegrini,
and Bobby Walston, who bought new houses in the Alden Park
development; Pedro Hernandez, arrested in 2013 for kidnapping
and strangling Etan Patz, 30 years after the boy appeared on the
backs of milk cartons; and Victoria Mae Budinger, "Miss Vicky,"
ex-wife of Tiny Tim, a Haddonfield native who at 17 married the
ukulele troubadour on The Tonight Show and owned a New Age
gift shop on Maple Shade's Main Street in the mid-1990s, and
who, in an instance of South Jersey fame crossover, was linked to
Fred J. Neulander, the Cherry Hill rabbi convicted of paying two
men to carry out a hit on his wife in 1994.

· · ·

Shaders worked hard and went home to work on their cars or
gardens. Or they went to a bar—there were so many bars along
one mile of Main Street (some records say 20, others 23 or 24) that
Maple Shade was rumored to appear in *The Guinness Book of World
Records*. It's a title many places claim: Bourbon Street in New

Orleans; George Street in St. Johns, Newfoundland; Market Street in Corning, New York; High Street in Clinton, Massachusetts; a few streets in Hoboken, New Jersey. *The Guinness Book of World Records* has never had such a section, but that never stopped Shaders from claiming the urban legend was true. I could have sworn Maple Shade could claim as its own one world-famous competitive eater of chicken wings, El Wingador.

I was wrong: El Wingador's from Woodbury Heights. Goes to show 'ya.

25.

Notes on WSLT

After a bike ride on the boardwalk, Dad and I stopped by the offices of WSLT, Ocean City, New Jersey. For the heck of it, Dad walked inside and asked about a DJ job. He met the station director, did a selection of his hokey DJ voices, and got a gig on the spot working Saturday nights. In 1980, just as the *Smokey and the Bandit* movie franchise gave Dad's trucker job a Hollywood flavor, the popularity of *WKRP in Cincinnati* made the idea of his being a DJ cool.

WSLT was an easy listening station, 1020 on the AM dial. More newscaster than DJ, Dad's new second job was swapping out Muzak reel-to-reels and taping a 90-second news report every hour. Not exactly a Johnny Fever who spun records and took listener calls. It didn't matter: I could brag to friends my dad was a radio DJ.

. . .

A couple months into his tenure, bored shitless, Dad started using his different voices. Dad's repertoire included at least four voices, complete with character names he announced on air: Jean-Paul Duvalier, a play on the name of Jean-Claude "Baby Doc" Duvalier, the iron-fisted president of Haiti; Bill Swithuns, an upper-class Englishman, reading news in BBC deadpan; Bruce Savage, a lispy gay male voice; and his favorite, Hans Überman, a play on philosopher Freidrich Nietzsche's "übermensch," a comic German accent that sounded like Dr. Strangelove. Dad presumed recording news in this manner would get him fired. But the programmers loved it.

. . .

I begged Dad to take me along. Dad resisted. It would be boring as hell, he said.

"I'll stay out of your way," I promised. "I'll bring my homework."

I packed a sleeping bag. Ocean City in the off-season was a ghost town, with traffic lights flashing yellow or red. As we stepped inside WSLT's office, I saw an Associated Press teletype machine, like from old movies. It cranked out a roll of paper in the middle of the room. Dad saw my eyes light up.

"Whatever you do," he said, "you do not touch that."

There was plenty not to touch. Reel-to-reel players took up a whole wall. In the back I found the real mother lode: boxes on the floor marked "trash," all filled with promotional 45s, tapes of public service announcements, and record flats. I wanted to take everything home.

"Just take a few," Dad said.

. . .

I made a stack of picture sleeve 45s, an odd assortment that included Squeeze's "Pulling Mussels from the Shell," Joan Armatrading's "Me Myself I," and The Normal's "TVOD," the B side of "Warm Leatherette," which I played constantly and pogoed to in my room. I begged Dad to bring records back for me each week. Until he quit a couple months later, he set up "Mike Nester's Box" by the coffee machine in the break room. A note asked for "any record you are going to throw away."

"My son will take anything," he wrote.

26.

Notes on the Lipstick Fights of Woodlawn Field

I tried on Meri's lipstick, just as a joke. It was Grandpop's birthday party. I wanted to make fun of Meri's new look, so I put on her lipstick and pranced around the house with her white pleather pocketbook. Everybody laughed. I went off to play basketball at the court behind our house. I forgot to wipe the lipstick off.

. . .

A bunch of grown men who still lived at home and filled pot-holes for the township hogged the court for more than an hour. Boys my age waited courtside. The sun was about to set, it was April and chilly, and they were running a full-court four-on-four. I bitched to one guy, Bobby Hollinger, as he dribbled past the three-point line.

"Can't you just play half-court?"

Bobby stopped, looked at me. Then he winged the basketball point-blank at my dick. The ball left a crater in my pants, like from a Road Runner cartoon. I fell down. The older guys laughed.

I stood up and, without thinking, took a swing at him. The left hook landed; his wire-rimmed John Denver glasses smacked onto the court.

I'd broken some rule or code. A child had hit a man.

• • •

Instead of trying to beat me up in turn—I realize now that he would've been arrested for that—Bobby called up his younger brother, David, to go after me, to "call me out," as we put it in Maple Shade. At 16, David Hollinger was still two years older than me and twice as big as his older brother. His biceps had big yellow veins usually seen on professional football linemen.

A week passed. Was it all just old man bluster? Was the hit he put on me called off? I wasn't taking any chances. I stayed inside. About a week later, back at the basketball court, David Hollinger and his veiny biceps walked onto the court in the middle of a game. He got right to the point.

"You punch my brother?" he asked. "Did you? Did you? You punch my brother?"

"Yeah, he threw a basketball at my balls," I said. My voice shook. "What else was I supposed to do?"

He swung a right punch and it landed on my eye. I fell. He kicked me in the ribs. He wore work boots. A small circle formed around us—older guys, little kids. I got back up one last time, and he punched me again, this time in the other eye. A coach came around and broke us up. I hobbled away, jumped over the back-yard fence, and went straight to bed.

If my social status in town wasn't already ruined, getting a public beatdown from a Big Jim lookalike sealed the deal.

• • •

The next morning, Dad inspected the two shiners and fat lip. He convinced me I needed to fight him again to, in his words, "regain my honor." The chance came at a family picnic the next week. I spotted the younger Hollinger behind our house playing pickup baseball in the CYO field. Before I hopped over the fence, Dad gave me a roll of pennies covered in electrical tape.

79

"This will make your punches feel like a rock," he said.

I put it inside my left hand. It felt solid. My courage grew. As I walked behind the baseball field, I breathed hard in my chest. I snuck behind a dugout and saw David standing in the batter's box. When he put the aluminum bat down, I ran up and jumped on his back. I put him in a headlock with my right arm and with my left hit his forehead with the penny roll. Nothing hurt him. He just got angrier. As he broke out of the hold, I bit his arm. He screamed.

"You're gonna bite me like a girl?"

I didn't care. I wanted to hurt him. I hit him with the penny roll's bare end in overhand swipes. Still didn't hurt him.

Dad and my Uncle Mark had walked over to the field. Hollinger broke from my hold and we stood by home plate, going toe-to-toe. He got hits in, but it didn't hurt. There was too much adrenaline; he could have punched me all day and it wouldn't have mattered.

"Hit him again!" Dad said, over and over.

Hollinger's friends tried to get in on the fight, but my Uncle Mark stopped them to keep it fair.

I bit his arm again. David walked backward out of the field, pointing two middle fingers.

"I'm comin' after you!"

• • •

Before there could be Bout Number Three, my Aunt Chrissy got a Hollinger sister she had gone to school with on the phone. "This has got to stop," I overheard her say. It took a 24-year-old woman to call another 24-year-old woman to call off a 22-year-old's hit on a 14-year-old by his 16-year-old brother. Fear mounts my neck writing about these fights, even now. Not because of the punches, or even the lipstick, or getting hit in the balls, but because there were so many other fights I've forgotten.

. . .

It's because of these fights that I first heard the story of Martin Luther King, Jr.'s visit to Maple Shade.

I was wearing contacts by then, the hard kind. During the second fight, a contact lens scratched my eye. I went to our family doctor, Dr. Sipstein, who kept his office just across from OLPH. Sipstein looked and sounded like a frog; he played this up with a collection of ceramic frogs, inflatable frogs, Hummel frogs, windup frogs, posters, plastic and rubber frogs given to him by family members and patients. He talked like Sammy Davis, Jr., slow and deliberate; we always thought he was drunk or on pills.

As Dr. Sipstein examined my eye, I told him how I was sick of fights, sick of not fitting in. Then he told me, matter of factly, how Martin Luther King, Jr. had gotten thrown out of a bar in town.

. . .

Left out of official town histories, the King story had been passed down by word-of-mouth. It is the height of adolescent vaingloriousness to say I identified my own cause with a Nobel Peace Prize-winner's fight against centuries of institutional racism and discrimination. I dared not express out loud this kinship with the civil rights leader; instead, I sang along to "Pride (In the Name of Love)," U2's King-inspired anthem. Teenage logic leaps swiftly and without fear.

27.

Notes on the Nester Curse

"Did you see that?"

"Did I see what?"

"Did you see how she gave me a little wink?"

"I think I did."

We had made our way to the McDonald's drive-through speaker, where Dad ordered in his serviceable English accent. This made the lady on the other end giggle a bit. We pulled around to get our food.

"Here you go," she said. Her voice sounded sweet. She wore a feather necklace and a Golden Arches cap tilted to the side. "Have a nice day."

That's when the girl gave a wink. At least I think she did.

Dad finger-flicked a Marlboro out the window and pulled into a spot to eat.

"That, my son, is called The Nester Curse. It's about time you got to know this, since you're about to enter manhood."

· · ·

The Nester Curse, Dad explained, stipulates that certain women—specifically older women, bigger women, black women—find Nester men irresistible.

"It might be our scent, the way we Nester men carry ourselves. Whatever the reason, these women throw themselves on us. All it takes is a twinkle in the eye, a smile, and that's it," he said. "Try not to lead women on."

. . .

I walked around thinking The Nester Curse was a real thing or hoping it was. I will admit here that, every once in a while, when a woman of a certain age or accent or size gives me a wink, I remember Dad's warning about The Curse.

28.

Notes on Mandy
(Or, Making Out in Church)

At least on paper—if we were good Freudians—I should be a foot fetishist. I say this because the first time that I ever got to second base—which, for international readers, is a slang for when some-one caresses a female's breasts—the petting began with foot play.

· · ·

Father McFadgen, our parish priest, took a few altar boys on a day trip to Bushkill Falls. Father McFadgen liked to take altar boys to far-flung places. One time he called Mom and asked to take me on a cross-country drive to New Mexico, just him and me. Mom made up some excuse, like we were going to go down the shore, but the truth was she thought letting her son stay in cheap hotels to see the Rocky Mountains with a 300-pound Roman Catholic priest didn't pass the smell test. At school we called him *Father McFaggin'* or *Father McFudgin'*, as in *packing fudge*.

· · ·

This was a group day trip, so Mom let me go. A girl came along, too: an eighth-grader named Mandy. I spent the drive to Bushkill talking to the other altar boys about CYO baseball. Mandy lay in the back cargo area holding hands with another eighth-grader, Sean Gilson. Whatever the opposite of an altar boy was, Sean Gilson fit the definition. He folded a pack of cigarettes into his t-shirt sleeve. A knife mark bisected his right eyebrow. In third grade, Sean beat every boy up in school, one by one, just to see if he could do it.

• • •

We were eating lunch at a picnic table by the falls. Since Mandy's name was Mandy, I sang a bit of Barry Manilow's "Mandy" to her—*I remember all my life, rainin' down as cold as ice.* Mandy took a shine to me. When the other altar boys weren't looking, Mandy deep-throated a french fry and looked at me. Then she dipped it in ketchup, and licked the fry up and down. I was aroused, but had no idea what it meant, let alone what to do about it. Dad's theory of The Nester Curse of attracting older women held weight after all.

• • •

Back in the station wagon, Mandy ditched Sean and invited me to join her in the station wagon's cargo area, just the two of us. I made it seem like a chore to lie in the back with a girl. Father McFadgen would have seen any hanky-panky in his rearview mirror, so Mandy resorted to below-sightline seduction with her feet. She slipped off her sneakers and ran her toes up and down my tube sock-covered calves. I remember lying there, trying at once to pretend nothing was happening, chitchatting with fellow acolytes, avoiding eye contact with her jilted psychotic lover, and at the same time giving as much of my attention as I could to Mandy's acrobatic feet.

• • •

When we got back to the rectory, we were supposed to call our parents for rides. Mandy and I wanted to pursue our romance further. Using Vince's janitor keys, I lured my tootsie tantalizer to an anteroom opposite the altar in the church, where Father

McFadgen put on his garments. It had one pew, an organ, and a line of candles. I laid down a robe in the corner and we proceeded to make out.

Mandy started to lick my teeth, systematically, incisors to molars, inside and out. Then I took her top off. Cable had just come to Maple Shade, and the whole scene seemed straight out a dirty movie I had just watched, *The Sensuous Nurse*. Shown late Saturday nights on Prism,[7] with Ursula Andress starring as the titular health care professional, the Sensuous Nurse gave old millionaires heart attacks when she flashed her boobs, then stole their money.

· · ·

I planted my mouth onto Mandy's breasts, licking them like a thirsty Labrador. And, before we go any further, I just want to say that if I noticed this detail now, it wouldn't be such a big deal. Here it is: Mandy's breasts were hairy. Really hairy. Long filaments encircled her nipples. I remember feeling repulsion while Mandy cooed, so loudly I had to muffle her mouth with my hand.

We heard doors opening and closing, the clink of more keys. Vince was making his rounds. I told her to run one way while I went in the other direction.

Mandy came and she gave without taking. And then I sent her away.

---

7   Philadelphia-area HBO knockoff station. Its offerings were limited to Phillies games and about thirty movies, half of which were Roger Moore-era James Bond.

29.

Notes on the German Question

To reach my Dad's copy of *Mein Kampf* required great struggle. Or at least a stepladder.

I called it Dad's *Nazi Stash*. Top shelf, all the way to the right, stacked like a grad student's bookend. *Is Paris Burning? The Arms of Krupp. The Rise and Fall of the Third Reich.* And of course, *Mein Kampf*.

I took down and kept *Sex and Society in Nazi Germany* for myself, its images of Teutonic orgies becoming the first porn I ever saw.

• • •

"After the Versailles treaty and the reparations, what did they expect?" he said. "Hitler brought back the German economy. Everyone was miserable."

As Laurence Olivier narrated episodes of *The World at War*, I was presented an alternative view of world history. I commemorated whichever battle we discussed with a pen and paper drawing. Always the terrain line first, maybe a mountain or hill to one side, tanks facing the right. Swastikas on the planes, flames and projectiles hitting them.

My father regarded Adolf Hitler as a Misunderstood Genius, and himself as someone who, had he lived in Germany in the 1930s, would have been an enthusiastic member of the Nazi Party.

"It's pretty simple," Dad explained as we watched France fall. "I am a Nationalist and a Socialist." He wrote words down on an index card. "I love the United States—it's the greatest country in the world. That means I am a Nationalist."

I sat Indian-style on the rug of our rec room. I nod. Of course this country is the Greatest. So I'm a Nationalist.

"I am also a Socialist. That means I believe in the sharing of wealth and labor."

I nod again. So I'm a Socialist.

"Nationalist-Socialist. Nazi. That's all a National Socialist means," he concluded.

• • •

Though I wouldn't have described him this way then, Michael Nester was a strange man, unsuitable for most social occasions. Except for his own wedding and his children's first communions and confirmations, he did not set foot inside OLPH or any other church. He disdained the faux pageantry of holidays, secular or religious, despised the quest for and installation of the Christmas tree, begrudged his role in the Easter egg hunt, squirmed amid regular-guy barbershop chitchat or sports talk. He abhorred peaceniks, hippies, earth children, corporate bigwigs and intellectuals equally. He preferred a Jack and Coke and cigarette in his chair, where he sat, reading, looking up, reading, looking up. He did not suffer other humans gladly.

•　•　•

Thirty years later, I put on one of my father's old German Military Marches records on my turntable. As the first track, "Dies Land Bleibt Deutsch!" ("This Land Remains German!"), begins, there's a scratch and hiss from the 78 transfer, then crashes of cymbals and brass, precise, completely without any swing. "Doesn't this music make you want to go out into battle?" he asked me back then, his hands gripping the armrests of his chair. He was 31 years old, and I was 11.

Notes on G. Gordon Liddy

"Give me three thousand G. Gordon Liddys," my father would say. "Just give me three thousand G. Gordon Liddys, and I could take over the world."

Dad's fascination with tough guys—Patton, Robert Duvall's Wagner-playing colonel in *Apocalypse Now*, the Dirty Harry movies—culminated in G. Gordon Liddy. I faintly recall Nixon resigning on TV. But I learned all I needed to know about Watergate from Liddy's autobiography, *Will*, which covered the 54 months he spent in jail, "the longest served by any of the Watergate participants."

Liddy overcame his childhood fears and transformed himself into a total badass. He cooked rats because he was afraid of them. He held his hand over a candle flame to demonstrate how he couldn't be made to talk. He sang German songs while taking a shower in jail. A television adaptation of *Will* starring tough guy actor Robert Conrad was an event in our house.

• • •

Inspired by Liddy's German-American upbringing in the mid-1930s, Dad led me through drills of straight-arm salutes, the "salute of Caesar's legions."

"Face your comrade." Dad put his right arm out. "Among warriors, the left hand would grab the other guy's balls. We won't do that."

We clicked heels at an angle. I raised my right arm and stuck it straight out. This, Dad pronounced, was the salute of our ancestors, the Barbarian salute of the Germanic peoples who brought down the Roman Empire!

Heil! Heil! we shouted at each other. *Hale! Hale!*

It felt like an episode of *Hogan's Heroes*. It didn't occur to me that we were doing Hitler salutes.

Mom walked in on us. She took one look at her husband and son mid-*Heil Hitler*-ing in the rec room.

"Oh, Jesus Christ, Mike, Danny," Mom said. "Cut it out. Time for dinner."

◆　◆　◆

All my life, I've tried to find an answer to what I call The German Question. Was my father really a Nazi? A Nazi enthusiast? Did he have some unnatural Nazi fascinations? I retold these stories to Mom thirty years later, and, while not quite disbelieving me, she said she didn't remember much of this.

"He seemed to think you would be interested," Mom said. "I never talked to him about that kind of Nazi stuff."

My mother's delivery—offhand, a little defensive, comic—distracted me from her meaning, which is to say that, on some level, I actually wanted to discuss the Third Reich with Dad, that these subjects might never have been brought up in conversation had my father not noticed his son's interest. Did I egg him on? If I am to be honest with myself, at the time I really was interested. I really did want to be taught about how my genes were superior to others.

My mother then turned to my wife.

"He was just so handsome," my mother said. "I just couldn't stop staring at him. Half the time I couldn't understand what he was saying. It didn't matter. I would just get lost in his blue eyes. I didn't know about this 'Hitler-German' business. I just thought he looked like James Dean and James Garner wrapped into one."

My wife nodded, bouncing our one-year-old on her lap.

31.

Notes on Deregulation

On July 1, 1980, President Jimmy Carter signed into law the Motor Carrier Regulatory Reform and Modernization Act, which opened the trucking industry to nonunion shops. "No longer will trucks travel empty because of rules absurdly limiting the kinds of goods a truck may carry," Carter said at the signing ceremony.

"Great," Dad said, as he watched Walter Cronkite's report. "Now any asshole with a rig and a bunch of amphetamines can do my job."

• • •

The Teamsters protested. If the Motor Carrier Act was passed, Robert F. O'Brien, the lawyer for my father's local, wrote in the *New York Times*, "for a portion of the population, it will wipe out substantial gains obtained as a result of a history of collective bargaining, particularly in New Jersey, which already is now experiencing more and more unemployment."

• • •

Deregulation. The word in our house meant *the end was near.* After Carter signed off on deregulation, my father and millions of other Teamsters like him never voted Democrat again.

The rumor mill at Dad's work heated up. The nights got slow; trucks left terminals half empty. Mom and Dad suffered what they called "panic attacks." Dad went on high-blood-pressure medication, and Mom, acting on her mother's advice, drank an Old Milwaukee each night before she went to bed.

Eddie Kentball, who got Dad the job 12 years before, stopped by the house one night.

"I'm fine," Eddie said, getting back into a shiny Buick LeSabre. "I've got seniority, and I'm on the way to retirement anyway. But it's the young guys like you, the ones with kids, that I worry about."

"I'm really confused about the future," I wrote in my journal.

· · ·

Years later, Mom said the periods of unemployment happened often. Dad was laid off several times over the years, usually in December, just in time for Christmas. When I think back to how my sister and I clamored over the years for a new Huffy bike or Barbie Glamour Camper Van under the Christmas tree, I want to crawl under a rock.

"Listened to President Ronald Reagan's State of the Union address this evening," I wrote on January 26, 1982. "He seems correct, but there's an element of something missing. I think he's being too impersonal toward the unemployed and elderly."

By mid-February, it was obvious this layoff was different. Dad went on call and collected unemployment. "We're ahead of the game," he told us. "Everything's ducky."

"Somehow I can't believe him," I wrote. "But as long as there's a roof over our heads and food on the table, we can make it."

· · ·

Weekdays, Dad was sprawled on the couch when I left for school in the morning and was still there each afternoon when I came home. Each morning, he called Boss-Linco and other companies to see about a day's work. To avoid losing a week's unemployment, he could only work up to three days in a single week; otherwise, his paycheck would not be as much as his unemployment,

93

and he would have to forgo the claim. To get back on the union rolls, Dad had to be called in for 30 days within a 90-day period. What happened, heartbreakingly, was that he got called in for 29 days and, on the 90th day, the phone sat silent. On day 91, we were back to square one.

. . .

Friends and family looked everywhere for leads on jobs. There were offers to work at a warehouse, another at Wawa. He refused to accept anything nonunion. "I'm not going to sweep a broom for five bucks an hour," Dad said.

"I'll work one more day at the school to help out," I wrote.

. . .

"He'd rationalize it with me, say he needed to keep his schedule open," Mom told me. It's 30 years later, a couple days after Christmas. Our girls climbed on Grandma Patti's lap. The fridge is full of kid snacks. It's starting to get awkward, asking Mom questions about her first husband, while Bill, her third, watches Eagles games on a recliner the next room over. The air grows just a little more thick and smoke-filled when I bring up the past. She'd let this all rest a long time ago, a whole life ago.

32.

Notes on Ass Ball

The generic term for the game is Wall Ball, but we played Ass Ball. Our Lady of Perpetual Help's Wall Ball variation—a mash-up of dodgeball and horse, with a dash of firing squad execution—required players to throw a tennis ball against the tall brick facade facing Poplar Avenue and keep score of whoever flubbed a catch. Ball-flubbers got an A, then an S, then another S. That spells ASS.

· · ·

Anyone with an ASS then assumed the position and faced the wall, bent-over with hands cupped over his crotch. The rest of us lined up to throw as hard as we could at the boy's ass. I still remember the hiss of tennis balls, the swack against my tailbone. Some boys lobbed, but others saw it as pitching practice and did their best Nolan Ryan imitations, windup and all.

As if this wasn't homoerotic enough, another variation, Dick Ball, got so far as Dwayne Spedman facing a firing squad, a social studies book in his pants. Sister Kathleen got wind and stormed across the rectory driveway, shouting in spondees, "GIVE YOUR BALLS TO ME, HONEY BUNNY!"

· · ·

One morning a tennis ball hit the leg of Jim Papper, the only black student in our class, maybe in all of OLPH. Kurt Youngblood, an ape of a boy who was left behind twice, saw the ball hit Papper's leg, then shouted, "Throw the ball at the nigger!"

Jim covered his head with his arms as balls rained down on him, then ran straight up to Kurt and punched him with overhand, wimpy blows. Kurt didn't even punch back; he just stepped aside and threw another tennis ball at him.

"Throw the ball at the nigger!" someone else shouted. "Hit the nigger!"

Papper went nuts and kept going at Kurt, like a bull in the ring. A crowd encircled them as they moved across the yard, Youngblood throwing away. Papper's head dripped blood and Kurt pelted him over and over again.

"STOP RIGHT NOW!" Sister Kathleen screamed. She grabbed Kurt's arm, raised to whale Papper with another throw. "You come with me now!"

• • •

"There was an incident in the schoolyard this afternoon that I will never see again," Sister Kathleen said over the PA. "Anyone who uses any racial insult—for example the n-word—will be punished and expelled."

She might have said the full n-word, and I have censored it retroactively in my memory. I think she did. Either way, a couple of the tougher dudes who joined in Papper's pelting giggled at its mention. I sat there, saying nothing, or maybe giggled along.

33.

Notes on a Survival Garden

It took until summer 1982 for the Boss-Linco Truck Lines to file for bankruptcy. Dad had been back working some nights. We held steady. Then the call from the Teamsters shop steward came. It was an afternoon in late July: we had just returned from a cross-country drive to Arizona to visit Dad's family. Our 1972 Country Squire station wagon was covered in stickers bearing the names of all the states we passed through.

· · ·

In my memory, it was that very day, with our luggage still strapped onto the car. Dad took the call in the bedroom. The door was open. He sat on the bed turned away from of us. It was hot outside.

He had a white tank top on, and his back was arched. He didn't say much on the phone: a couple of *yups* and *rights*. At some point, he stood up, turned around, and spoke to us. The news didn't sink in completely, not right then. It was the first time I thought of my father as broken, let alone breakable.

· · ·

Even now I'm all like: *Fuck you, deregulation. You started all this.*
Even now I'm all like: *Jimmy Carter, elder statesman?*

• • •

Mom and Dad talked in the backyard while Meri and I listened in, standing on the rec room couch. Dad called up a trucking place for work and identified himself as "Miguel Nester," a Mexican version of himself, in the hope that he would be taken on as an affirmative action hire. This tactic did not pan out. Neither did his letter to Vice-President George Bush, in which he asked for a job drilling for oil at his son George Jr.'s fledgling business venture in Midland, Texas.

• • •

At first the unemployment thing seemed fun. We rented a tiller and dug up a "Survival Garden," as we called it, a 90-square-foot plot with rows of tomatoes, carrots, peppers, lettuce, radishes, zucchini, even a few cornstalks in the back, which turned out to be a variety meant for horses that I ate anyway. We dove into Sea-Lect Seafood's dumpster to pick out fish heads, which Dad had read made great fertilizer. As we planted them into the ground, Meri and I sang "Fish Heads," a novelty song I had taped off the Dr. Demento show. At night, our dog, Snuffy, dug them out.

• • •

Mom got a job waitressing job at Merchantville Country Club, where Uncle Frank had taken over the food concession. One night, two older men in plaid pants asked if she "wanted to look at their van." My mother, not usually the most street-smart lady, nevertheless declined.

"When I said 'no thanks,' the tip they left was a dime," she remembers now.

Everyone knew Dad was depressed. He went on a diet of crackers and canned sardines, the cheapest he could find, which, combined with the fish-head-smelling dog, made the kitchen stink like a seafood market aisle.

. . .

"There is little sympathy felt in this world of rhetoric for the silent sufferings of the genteel poor," Edmund Gosse wrote, "yet there is no class that deserves a more charitable commiseration."

. . .

A book on the coffee table around this time, mentioned here for foreshadowing purposes: *Clean Slate: A State-by-State Guide to Expunging an Arrest Record.*

34.

Notes on Guilt and Grace

There seemed to me back then an infinite number of ways to feel guilty. I broke down the varieties of guilt-filled experience into a table that cross-referenced different Cardinal sins with one another. I played this game of Sin Bingo in my head all through seventh and eighth grade:

B	I	N	G	O
LUST: Stare at clarinet player's butt	GLUTTONY: Eat half gallon of ice cream after thinking about clarinet player's butt	GREED: Steal uncle's *Penthouse*	SLOTH: Lazy day of dirty thoughts; repeated listens to Berlin's "Sex (I'm A)"	WRATH: Throw rocks while thinking of clarinet player's butt
ENVY: Jealous of non-rock-throwing boys who are attracted by the clarinet player's butt	PRIDE: Think about masturbation	LUST: Stare at *Hustler* hidden inside tree fort in woods	GLUTTONY: Drink Dad's 2-liter Coke while he's away at work	GREED: Steal quarters from Mom's purse to play Asteroids
SLOTH: Watch Bugs Bunny cartoons all day	WRATH: Kill things with BB gun	GUILT-FREE SPACE	ENVY: Kids with leather, not canvas, high-top sneakers	PRIDE: Wear ace bandage around waist to hide love handles

And so on. This might indicate that I focused on one sin at a time. More accurate: I felt as if I committed all possible sins at all possible times.

• • •

It's not like I did anything especially sinful at 12 years old. By seventh grade I regarded myself as a biblical scholar, complete with multiple crucifixes and rosary bead sets, pamphlets on each book from the Old and New Testaments.

• • •

In Catholic school, you are taught to be a child in the eyes of God. After a while, this didn't make sense to me. Why grow up to be an adult if, in the end, our goal was to be childlike? Why make the transition to adulthood ever? Asking these questions only made me feel guiltier.

• • •

I started to be, at my most devout, skeptical. I realized guilt was mundane, as repetitive as it was universal. It's as if I had been trying to drive the guilt out of my system before I was able to commit anything truly guilt-worthy.

35.

Notes on Grief:
Conspiracy Theories

The night after Meri called to say Dad died, I watched TV in the dark. My brand of insomnia is usually spent online, reading comment threads, checking out slideshows of movie stars, writing comments on blogs dedicated to rock bands.

. . .

Flicking channels, I caught the tail end of *Conspiracy Theory*. In one scene, Julia Roberts kneels at a fresh grave, the dirt fluffy and brown. The grave is for Mel Gibson's character, an obsessive New York cabbie who had fallen in love with Roberts, a government worker. She takes off her sunglasses, revealing tears. The camera pulls back to reveal Arlington Cemetery's rows and rows of military headstones. I was just about to cry for the first time since my father's death when Julia Roberts appears onscreen, riding a horse in full equestrian gear.

An SUV drives up and it's Mel Fucking Gibson. He's still alive.

. . .

"He wasn't really a father!" Meri had instant-messaged me years ago. "He was this creature who lived inside our house!"

. . .

Over the years, I have brought out of storage all the boxes of books Dad left behind. I put them all on a shelf, an approximation of the rec room's old arrangement. I take out his old LPs and lean them against a speaker. I'd sit in a ragged yard-sale chair and flip through his index cards, his journals.

◆ ◆ ◆

His books show a fascination with classic conspiracy theories: The Rothschilds, the Warburgs, J. P. Morgan and the Rockefellers, the *Anglo-Saxon frontmen for the Jewish banking industry*. I find several copies of Gary Allen's *None Dare Call It Conspiracy*, which he handed out to friends and family.

"Do you see how he really claimed to be agnostic?" Aunt Chrissy said to me once. "He probably didn't even realize it, but what he was reading added up to a kind of spirituality. The whole transformation, transfiguration, I'm-going-to-change-my-life stuff. It's admirable."

◆ ◆ ◆

He was asking you questions to prepare you for when he left. He wanted to toughen you up. He kept his distance so you wouldn't miss him when he left.

◆ ◆ ◆

I obsessed over what he wrote in the margins. Most of my father's notes from 1969–1982 are about reshaping the way one views the physical world. In his copy of Norman O. Brown's *Life Against Death: The Psychoanalytical Meaning of History*, my father's annotations center around the idea of a conscious self that controls and represses our desires.

Big brackets around Plato's doctrine: the "fundamental quest of man is to find a satisfactory object for his love." Instead of Freud's "pleasure-principle," Brown writes later, we have the "reality-principle." Brown throws Schopenhauer's notion of the "primacy of will" into the pot, and my Dad's marks go crazy. This idea of *will* stands in marked contrast with what Brown classifies as "seceding from the great, and really rather insane, Western tradition that the goal of mankind is to become as contemplative as possible."

Then, at the top of one page, my father writes:

EAST IS EAST AND WEST IS WEST?????
EAST IS WEST AND WEST IS EAST;
AND NEVER THE TWAIN SHALL CLEAVE?"

Was my father the West and my mother the East in the logic of my father's marginalia? Where's the *twain*? What's to *cleave*?

·   ·   ·

He wrote down definitions. From the "Sources of Plato's Opinions" section in Bertrand Russell's *A History of Western Philosophy*:

Teleology – 1. The study of final causes. 2. The fact or quality of being directed toward a definite end or of having an ultimate purpose, especially attributed to natural purposes. 3. A belief, as that of vitalism, that natural phenomenon are determined not only by mechanical causes but by an overall design or purpose in nature. 4. The study of evidence for this belief.

Underlined in Will Durant's *The Story of Philosophy*: a passage about the Greeks' "disdain of manual work."

·   ·   ·

A page with its corner folded has an underlined passage explaining Friedrich Nietzsche's famous "God is dead" idea.

DEAD ARE ALL THE GODS: NOW DO WE
DESIRE THE SUPERMAN TO LIVE.

. . .

Multiple underlinings in Ayn Rand, Voltaire, Hegel, Albert Einstein's *Out of My Later Years*, Aldous Huxley's *Brave New World*.

In *The Crack in the Cosmic Egg: Challenging Constructs of Mind & Reality*, John Chilton Pearce writes about how belief in a higher being can provide a "faith projection."

"A change of world view," he writes, and which my father teleologically double-underlines in deep-set pen-strokes, "can change the world viewed."

. . .

Before he died, he had been sick for years, estranged from his first and second batch of kids. At first, when I missed my father, I missed him terribly. It was a bodily ache. I imagined hugging him, his torso and mine meeting, a squeeze that took air out of my lungs. His whiskers.

I remembered my attempts at dead-lifting him off the ground, my arms around his chest.

. . .

The news spread quickly through my mother's family. My Aunt Chrissy, on her Facebook page, summed up my family's reaction. "How do you mourn someone who was a part of our lives, part of some of the best laughs, part of the best people I love, and who has not been a part of our lives for so long?"

I didn't know how to answer that question, but I almost cried watching Julia Roberts cry.

Notes on Switching Bishops

"Maybe I'm outright paranoid," I wrote on May 22, 1982 (part II), "but people are starting to treat me like an outsider." After OLPH, kids went to either Maple Shade High School or Holy Cross High School. I had a definite opinion on the matter.

"I don't want to go to Maple Shade High School," I wrote. "I'm afraid if I have good grades, they'll beat me up. But times are tough and we may not be able to afford Holy Cross. At MSHS they'll kick my butt. Oh God, please don't let me go to Maple Shade. It will be a living nightmare, and I'm not being dramatical [sic] at all."

• • •

"Holy Cross is too expensive," Mom finally admitted. "They want the whole tuition at the beginning of the year."

I offered to help. The Moped Fund, I explained, could turn into the Dan Goes to Catholic School and Doesn't Get His Ass Beat Fund.

"We'd be so proud of you," she said. "The thing is, we might not be able to help from our end."

• • •

At work, I lit votive candles and prayed I wouldn't end up walking the same hallways as the Hollingers and Youngbloods, kids who would later wind up in jail for dealing coke in the Navy or show up on my Facebook feed puffed up from steroids.

Mom breathed a sigh of relief when Meri, her mouth full of costly orthodontia, announced her intention to go to Maple Shade High School. I still held out for a miracle. Sister Kathleen saved the day.

"Patti," she said to my mother, "have you considered sending Danny to Camden Catholic?"

Just four miles down Route 38, Camden Catholic was closer than Holy Cross but in another diocese. I had never thought anyone cared about allegiances to bishops.

Camden Catholic was "just as good" as Holy Cross, Sister Kathleen said, "maybe even better." I had heard Holy Cross's principal was a tyrant. But what sealed the deal was that Camden Catholic had a monthly payment plan.

.   .   .

There were no uniforms for boys at Camden Catholic: just a dress code of dress slacks, shirt, and a tie. This, Mom determined, would be an added expense, but I promised to buy my own clothes and lunches as well as help with the $157 monthly payments.

And here we have our second-act twist. Not quite a cliffhanger, but definitely a change of setting, four miles away, in another diocese, another county, another world.

ACT TWO

37.

Notes on Grief

I chickened out. I'd promised my sister that I would go to Arizona. But I chickened out. I didn't want to go back to Tucson, where my father lived since I was 17. There would be no service, no burial, no headstone or wake. I had a family vacation to Vermont planned the next week. So I chickened out.

. . .

Is there such a thing as grieving without grief? What I mean is: without a specific object for grief, what is grieving called?

To "come to grief" implies time or a process. *Getting to grief. Giving someone grief.*

I think: I didn't *arrive* at grief.

. . .

No one *gave* me grief anyway. Grief came to me, gradually, eventually. Grief, from the Latin *gravare*, "to make heavy," as in *gravity* or *grave* or *grievance*.

Grief weighs me down. If I still talked to God, I am sure any grief without an object would still have anger and emptiness, a tightness in my chest.

I'd feel just as childish and heavy and whiny. I'd be angry with God.

As it stands, I'm angry in my grief.

38.

Notes on Mary's Café:
Toward a Shader Ethos

"For lack of a beer—King rocked America's bias," proclaimed the title of an article in Ohio's *Chronicle-Telegram*. Published on January 17, 1976, it marked the passing of Ernest Nichols, owner of Mary's Café. "As thousands around the country marked the 47th anniversary of Dr. King's birth with special commemorative services and rallies," the story reads, "the bartender who ordered Martin Luther King, Jr. and his friends out of his tavern was buried in a quiet ceremony in Riverside, N.J."

Only three newspaper mentions of King's encounter at Mary's Café have appeared in the past half century. This was one of them.

• • •

"I've been in town 27 years, and it's one of those things people talk about," a township clerk told the *Philadelphia Inquirer* in 1988 ("The Bar That Began a Crusade"). "It's becoming a fable. Of course it gets all bent out of shape. Whatever happened, it's not something people are proud of, to tell you the truth."

Is it possible to be *unproud of a fable?*

• • •

"No one gave much thought at all" to the King incident, W. Thomas McGann explained to the *Philadelphia Inquirer*. As a young lawyer, McGann defended Nichols in the civil rights and criminal complaints. Then, in 1968, "some senator asked Dr. King what had stimulated his interest in civil rights and he recounted what had happened to him in what he said was the suburbs of Camden."

I can't find the record of King's exchange with some senator, but it is true that no mention of Mary's Café turns up until 1970. McGann went on to become Burlington County's Superior Court Judge. In 1976, he spoke more frankly about his role in defending Ernest Nichols.

"I don't think it was a question of Nichols not wanting to serve them," he recalled. "Negroes were served at his bar. But as I recall, he was very defensive about the incident. His tavern was frequented by blue collar workers, and Dr. King and his companions were different than the ordinary folk. They spoke a better language, used better diction."

If there *were* such a thing as a Shader Ethos, it would need to include a wariness of fancy-talking, unordinary folk.

◆ ◆ ◆

The King who drove into Maple Shade in 1950 had not yet become the Martin Luther King, Jr. who led the Montgomery Bus Boycott five years later. King had not yet figured out his true calling. In 1950, an unnamed evaluator assessed King at Crozer Theology School, and listed his weaknesses as an "attitude of aloofness, disdain, and possible snobbishness which prevent his coming to close grips with the rank and file of ordinary people."

39.

Notes on My Crucifixion

My Jesus Freak stage reached its apex on Good Friday, April 9, 1982.

    • • •

The story begins a few weeks earlier. I had finished mopping the church basement. The day was sunny, the classrooms clean, and I drank a Click Root Beer outside on the curb. Sister Kathleen spotted me.

"Can I ask you a question, Daniel?" Sister Kathleen's voice sounded even lower, more solemn than usual.

"Sister K, you haven't been traded, have you?"

She laughed at this baseball term I used when nuns got transferred to other parishes. We'd become friends. I hoped she was staying. She sat down on the curb.

"No, Daniel, it's not that. I would like to ask you a question." She paused, took in an audible breath. "What would you think about playing Our Lord Jesus Christ in the Passion Play?"

    • • •

I was not a fan of our annual Passion Play, which I regarded as a Vegas-style dinner theater desecration. Typecasting also concerned me. Each designated Jesus Junior entered the pantheon of wimpy cherubs who committed in the eyes of other students the ultimate act of brownosery: playing the Son of God.

I didn't need this kind of extra attention. In a few weeks I'd be out, and the less people noticed me, the better. At the same time,

I didn't want to sound rude and reject the role outright without giving a good reason, especially to the nun who helped me find my new high school.

"To tell you the truth," I told her, looking down on the concrete, "I don't think I'm worthy."

. . .

This statement of false humility, unintentionally pitch perfect, made me more of a lock for the role. I could tell the second those words came out of my mouth.

So I told Sister Kathleen that I would be honored to play Our Lord.

. . .

When I went home to tell the news, Mom cried. "I'm so proud of you," she said. "You'll be playing our Messiah!"

Dad the unrepentant agnostic gave his two cents. "So, you're Jesus?" He chuckled, blew out smoke. "You know what that makes me, right?"

. . .

We had rehearsals, learned marks to hit, gestures to make. By Good Friday, I had the whole impersonating the Prince of Peace thing down. "My kingdom is not of this world," my trombone teacher intoned from the choir loft, and I pointed both arms toward the heavens. As Pontius Pilate, Robby Smart, fresh from the hairstylist with a new perm that made him look vaguely Roman, hammed it up as he condemned me to death. Simon, played by Tommy Branthardt, helped me up with my Styrofoam cross as I fell three times. And the role of Mary Magdalene, in a perfect casting choice, was played by Marie Rocco. Marie's curves had only ripened since our kiss on April 14, 1977. It's a date I can verify because it coincided with the day the Garden State Racetrack burned down. Dark smoke rose into the sky while we smooched.

We should have taken it as a sign that something was amiss. We broke up the next day.

Seventh-graders stripped me down to a loincloth sewn into tighty whities. The marble floor chilled my bare feet. I remained still up on the cross, arms spread in cruciform pose, through the choir's ultra-Caucasian take on "Were You There When They Crucified My Lord?"

Grandmom wept through the whole thing, holding Mom's hand.

• • •

Here's what I wrote the morning after:

> April 10, 1982. Holy Saturday today. I didn't make any mistakes in the Passion Play yesterday and did pretty good. I took a glimpse of a TV show with William F. Buckley, Jr. He was talking to some really interesting professor of philosophy. They were talking about angels. They said they could move without taking up time or space. That's like if I moved from A→B without taking up time. That's also like if you're everywhere at once but your [sic] only conscious of the places you want to be. These things really dumbfounded me.

The episode of *Firing Line*, "In What Sense Are Humans Angelic?", resolved to find "the distinction between angels and the present company." Guests Ernest van den Haag and Mortimer Adler debated the angelic occupation of space and the "theology of electrons." Back then, I wanted to believe that angels floated among us, that I could be an angel, that I could be everywhere at once.

116

Notes on Car Washes

My last childhood bike resembled a circus clown's. Made from scraps of previous bicycles left around the garage, it had long handlebars, a small tire up front and large one in back, a flower-patterned banana seat, and one of those orange safety flags mounted behind a four-foot sissy bar. I'd like you to picture a 14-year-old boy as he rode this monstrosity three miles down a hill along a two-lane county road, where Main Street turns into East Camden Avenue, just past Mary's Café, where Maple Shade bunches up and cracks at its borders, before the road goes black and smooth.

This was my commute to Sunshine Wash 'n Buff, my second job. In October of my freshman year, Dad got a tip from another truck driver, "Captain Midnight," who earned his handle racking up hours of overtime. His son, Bill, managed a car wash in Moorestown. They were "looking for wipers," people who toweled off cars as they came off the track.

"Show up Saturday morning," Dad said. "They say they'll have work for you."

• • •

No one said hello as my biked fishtailed onto the lot. Just an old man with leathery skin and a cigarette precipiced on his lips. His name was Buck.

"Take two of those," Buck said. He pointed to a shopping cart filled with towels. "Watch what I do on my side, and you do the same."

Buck came straight out of central casting as Wizened Old Man #1, a Harry Dean Stanton type with a long scar on his neck. As I thrashed my arms around the bodies of those first cars—bumper, hood, windshield, side, windows, trunk, bumper—I realized that Buck and I made up the "Buff" part of Sunshine Wash 'n Buff's operation.

Our most important job was minding the tips, a plastic five-gallon bucket set on top of cinder blocks with "THANKS" spelled out in duct tape. After each wipe-down, we waited for drivers to roll down their window and throw something in there, at which point we thanked them profusely and gave their rear bumper an extra wipe.

I tried some awkward line of conversation with Buck, but he pointed to his ear, then the blower at the end of the track.

"Can't fucking hear over that!" he shouted. In my memory, he sounds exactly like William S. Burroughs. The only time Buck ever said anything was when someone in a BMW or Mercedes threw pennies in the tip bucket.

"Jerk-offs," Buck growled when he heard the pennies plink. "Real fucking jerk-offs."

◆ ◆ ◆

We washed 500 cars that day, about average for weekends. My arms, noodle-tired, throbbed as we wiped down the last bumper. We counted up coins and bills from the tip bucket.

"How'd I do?" I asked, anxious for approval.

Buck's eyes met mine for the first time since morning. He took a drag off a Lucky Strike. "We got 'em through, didn't we?"

And that's how my professional car-washing career began.

• • •

From 1982 to 1987, all through my high school years and beyond, if you drove by Sunshine Wash 'n Buff on Camden Avenue in the Lenola section of Moorestown, summers or on weekends, chances are you'd have seen a skinny guy with fluffy yellow hair motioning to drivers to pull up, then wiping down the passenger side.

• • •

Sunshine's owner, Luigi, an Italian Stallion from Pennsauken, pulled up each night and flashed his brights to collect the day's take. His work boots were immaculate; his battleship-gray Lincoln Continental glowed under the streetlights, his windshield spotless, his tires jet-black. Luigi collected money belts from the managers of his three locations and counted the bills in the warmth of his car, denominations piled separately on his dashboard. He then handed each of us a damp roll of bills for our pay. We got four dollars an hour. Luigi got to keep half of the money from the tip bucket, which I am fairly certain was illegal. We split the other half. On really busy days in the winter, I'd make almost a hundred dollars.

I can think of another benefit: my complexion improved. I was now spending time in this place called "the outdoors," and my acne went away from all that Vitamin D. My biology teacher once asked if I went to the Caribbean on weekends, observing my winter face tan.

• • •

All the dudes who worked there got baked off their gourds. The crew smoked pot in the morning as cars lined up outside, holding in hits until the first customer closed their windows. I was the youngest person there by at least ten years, and I think that's partly why they didn't pressure me to get high. I remained morally opposed to marijuana. It was expected as a car wash colleague, however, that I would pass joints around. It's been more than 20 years, but I can still smell the bouquet of marijuana resin inside a car wash's soap-sterile mist. I can see now how a car wash is perhaps the most stoner-friendly job in the world: car after car, tire after tire, bumper after bumper, stereo up all the way, the track's hum, the side brush pirouettes, the wooly mammoth-looking roof brush, which my youngest daughter now calls "the sudsy octopus."

The U.S. unemployment rate approached 10 percent by late 1982. Many of my wiping partners were unemployed truckers. Some had kids. Others had separated from their wives.

$$\bullet \quad \bullet \quad \bullet$$

A couple years later, I found out the real story behind my first day. It seemed that Captain Midnight had told my father about the job so Dad could make some extra money under the table. Dad, however, dispatched me to work there instead. At the end of my first day, when Bill and the other guys walked up from the back, they were surprised to find a 14-year-old boy wiping cars with old man Buck. They said I could stick around.

41.

Notes on the Bon Jovi Incident

I'd resigned myself to being outsmarted by my younger sister. Until the Bon Jovi Incident.

It began when Meri got dropped off by a different group of boys, and in a different car, than the group that had picked her up. This occurred after Meri obtained special permission from Mom to go to Bratz, a local rock club, to see an unknown band called Bon Jovi.

◆ ◆ ◆

This was years before Bon Jovi's big break with "Wanted Dead or Alive." Their hit around this time was "In and Out of Love," but an older song, "Runaway," remained my sister's favorite. As best as I could tell, "Runaway" tells the story of a girl who dresses very much like my sister and works as a prostitute. Meri played "Runaway" constantly. Its synth intro pierced the wall between our rooms.

◆ ◆ ◆

Minutes after Meri came home, I heard Mom shouting.

"You've got the goods!"

I cracked my door open so I could witness my younger sister actually get in trouble. Mom wagged her index finger, and Meri stood in front of her, arms crossed, stone-faced. She had super-tight acid-wash jeans, a matching denim jacket gathered at the waist that made her torso look V-shaped, and white leather boots. I knew that, deep inside her Le Sports Sac, she had beer bottles slipped inside Wigwam socks to muffle their clinking.

"Are you listening to me? You've got the goods!"

"The "goods" my mom spoke of comprised my sister's virginity, honor, boobs, or some combination of the three. Mom stressed that she had these "goods" to indicate that they can somehow be, respectively, taken, lost, or groped.

•   •   •

It wasn't just the fact that she stayed out late and got a ride home from a different set of boys. This talking-to in the living room occurred after Meri had been caught with a joint. A marijuana cigarette! Inside her V-shaped denim jacket!

The only time Mom ever smoked pot, ever smelled it even, happened with Dad just after both of us were born. Mom and Dad sat in the backyard smoking a doobie, drinking Blue Nun wine. Then a lightning storm came, and that was all it took to freak Mom out. She never tried it again.

My mother thought my sister was drugged and abducted by Bon Jovi fans and dropped off on our front lawn.

The jig is up, I thought. Meri Nester was finally getting her due.

•   •   •

And here's exactly when I gave up all hope of ever getting away with anything: my sister got off scot-free.

Why? I'll tell you why. She used The Greg Brady Defense. It was so transparent to me when it happened, but Mom never saw it coming. Oh, I'm sorry: you're not familiar with The Greg Brady Defense? I'll remind you. The Greg Brady Defense comes from the episode "Where There's Smoke" (Season 2, Episode 14) of the acclaimed family dramedy *The Brady Bunch*.

Greg, the oldest brother, meets up with some friends who want him to join their "hard rock" band, The Banana Convention. As they talk, they offer him a cigarette, which Greg puffs on and coughs while he tries to act cool. The Brady sisters—Marcia, Jan, Cindy—see this and narc on Greg. He admits to smoking a cigarette, but the Brady parents don't punish him, rewarding Greg for his honesty.

Later in the episode, a whole pack of cigarettes falls out of Greg's jacket. Now everybody thinks he's really in trouble, including Greg, but get this: he says it's not his jacket, it's someone else's. What's more, Mr. and Mrs. Brady believe him. So he's off the hook.

"If I was in your place, I'm not sure I'd believe *me*," Greg says.

In Greg Brady's case, it truly wasn't his jacket. In my sister's case, it was.

· · ·

Patti Nester was relieved to find out her daughter wasn't a pot-smoking prostitute who listened to Bon Jovi; that she was, instead, a Bud pony-drinking, 16-year-old girl who merely dressed like a prostitute and listened to Bon Jovi. Now that she'd given her daughter the female empowerment speech, Meri got off with time served.

I cracked open my door to see Meri saunter back to her room. She smiled, gave me the finger, and shut the door.

42.

Notes on Cherry Hill

Drive around South New Jersey and you'll pass through some of the richest and poorest towns in the country. This wide gap is spanned by my high school's full name: Camden Catholic High School Cherry Hill.

"I never thought about sending you to Camden Catholic," Mom said. "Just the name got me nervous." Not the whole name, really, but one word in the name: "Camden." One of the poorest and most dandgerous cities in the country, Camden warded off most parents of OLPH eighth-graders. Black people lived in Camden, after all, and just the prospect of going to school with black kids was enough to shoo Shaders away.

Tacked on to the school's name by a vice principal in the early 80s, the words Cherry Hill reminded people of the school's actual location. It signaled to suburban parents that Camden Catholic was Camden in name only. Cherry Hill, a land of robust household incomes and swim clubs, described in an urban planning textbook as the "quintessential postmodern New Jersey suburb," is more idea than place. Sprawled around swim clubs and synagogues and bivouacs of faux colonials, Cherry Hill also provided half of Camden Catholic's kids.

• • •

The best way to explain Cherry Hill is that it was named after a mall. Built in 1961 on a plot beside Route 38, The Shops at Cherry Hill was the first indoor shopping center east of the Mississippi.

Touted as a majestic public planning experiment, the mall was built with 14,000 trees, flowers, and shrubs, and 110 skylights. The central area had the same dimensions as Philadelphia's cathedral-like 30th Street Station.

Shortly before it opened, an assistant to the mall's architect expressed concern that visitors would be too distracted to shop, instead staring up at the water fountain geysers shooting twenty-some feet into the air.

"The people should not be raising their eyes," the architect replied, "save to the Lord for our creating for them such an attractive and wonderful place."

◆ ◆ ◆

Camden Catholic culture shock started on Day One in September 1982. For reasons never explained, the bus company combined the routes for Maple Shade and West Camden. The bus looked like a scene from *The Warriors*: a boombox that blasted Michael Jackson, Grandmaster Flash, Cold Crush Brothers, Fearless Four. Black girls tried on each other's gold-hooped earrings. I was not in Maple Shade anymore.

◆ ◆ ◆

"I came well-dressed, feeling out the apparel of my peers," is what I wrote in my journal. "The next day I dressed a bit more informally, as my acquaintances, old and new, became more and more comfortable."

Did I think I lived in an Edith Wharton novel?

◆ ◆ ◆

I kept my chin up. "I seem to be emerging as a force to be dealt with," I wrote. "I have a few girls that [sic] like me. At dances I do fairly well. I seem to be 'making it' there." Then I seem to be emulating Margaret Mead: "The social structure is fast closing with circles and I seem to fall in [a] couple."

. . .

Girls from Cherry Hill—how to describe them? Thick-thighed, shoulder-padded Amazons in fingerless gloves. Lifeguard-certified, leg-warmered preppy-sprites. Each girl smelled nice and was pretty.

43.

Notes on the Testosterone Shots

In 1962, Dr. Murlin Nester administered injections of testosterone enanthate to his son, 13-year-old Michael. The reason given for the treatments by Dr. Nester was to "speed things up." In today's medical literature, the diagnosis for testosterone shots is "delayed puberty."

The treatment was relatively new, developed by chemists in postwar Germany who combined steroids with hog bile and other agents. Dr. Nester's regimen for his son lasted more than a year, and whatever was delayed, judging by family photos, sped up quickly. In one picture, dated 1963, Michael is a shiny-cheeked cherub; in his 1964 high school yearbook, he's six inches taller, a greaser with a pompadour and sideburns.

◆ ◆ ◆

The most obvious effect we acscribed to Dad's year of hormone shots was his all-over body hair, which at the beach made him look like Chewbacca with sunglasses. A coat of hair spanned his lower back, upper arms, and shoulders. "That motherfucker Nester," one of Dad's coworkers said, "he looks like an ape. He's got hair *on the back of his hands*."

As he came out of the Atlantic Ocean, lifeguards gawked at the seaweed that clung to Mike Nester's back hair. Little girls ran to their blankets, screaming, *sea monster, sea monster!*

◆ ◆ ◆

I offer this as background for the next set of Notes.

44.

Notes on Camden Catholic High School's 1983 Freshman Morp

May 1983. I'd been asked to Camden Catholic's freshman morp dance[8] by Melissa Donatucci, a five-foot-two, extremely busty girl from my Latin class. With money from the car wash, I bought an irregular suit from Marshall's and Ambervision sunglasses.

• • •

Before Dad left for work, he walked into the living room for what he called "the inspection."

"Tie knot, check. Shoeshine, check."

He then placed his briefcase on the coffee table—I have yet to meet another Teamster who carried an attaché—clicked it open, and produced three white capsules.

"These are zinc supplements," he said, then handed them to me. "They increase your virility."

Over the years, Dad had put me on regimens of various supplements—bee pollen, kelp, shark marrow, flavonoids, and coenzymes—ordered from the back pages of *Mother Earth News*. It was all part of his quest to transform me into a Nietzschean Überman who would vanquish the self-perpetuating clique of leaders we read about, Masonic-Jewish welders of Hegelian dialectics with Feuerbachian materialism.

---

8 Morp is prom spelled backward, and so girls asked out the boys, who were considered not yet ready to ask girls out to dances.

I just went with it. Doesn't every son want to please his father?

He then tucked three Trojan Naturalamb condoms into my jacket pocket. "And these are for protection."

It was not lost on me, even at 14, that I had been given a supplement to increase the volume of my ejaculate and the means to contain said ejaculate, all in one kit for my evening.

Dad offered one last piece of advice.

"Remember, son," he said, pointing at me, "Italian girls are not for marriage. They are for recreational purposes only."

• • •

Uncle Frank, my Aunt Terry's husband, pulled his white Cadillac Fleetwood into our driveway. That night marked his debut as chauffeur for high school formals. He wore a tuxedo t-shirt from Spencer's, a chauffeur's cap, and a full-length, black leather jacket. He resembled the touring keyboardist for The Gap Band.

Uncle Frank had brought along his high school buddy, Jimmy Jeffers. Frank and Jimmy passed a flask around as we drove to Melissa's house.

"So I hear your date has big bazongas," Jimmy said, turning his head around to the back seat. "How big do you think they are?"

"I don't know," I said. "I don't know girls' bra sizes or anything like that."

"You don't need to," Jimmy said. "Just show us with your hands."

I cupped my hands over my chest.

"Holy shit," Frank shouted from the rearview mirror. "That's at least 36D. You're in business!"

They high-fived.

. . .

I knew, well before this exchange, that Frank could guess women's bra sizes. Frank also possessed a special power whereby he could pick the class tramp out of any high school yearbook.

Frank had a perm and mustache. He brought mirrored shades and binoculars to the beach. He bequeathed to me his collection of *Cheri* magazines and Seka videocassettes.

By day, Frank sold meat. He drove to the Philly waterfront, picked up steaks and lobsters, put them in white boxes, wrote things like "Surf and Turf: Le Bec-Fin" on them, put the boxes in his Toyota truck, its bed chest filled with dry ice, and sold meat door-to-door to Bryn Mawr housewives.

What I am trying to say is: Frank was my idol.

. . .

As we made our way through the Camden Catholic parking lot, Frank and Jimmy peeked in the rearview mirror at Melissa, who wore a Madonna-inspired white dress that fit like a corset. The dance progressed in its usual way—white people pogo-danced to "Rock Lobster," black people break-danced during "Planet Rock," and dorks like me did Eddie Van Halen air guitar to "Beat It."

For the finale, "Always and Forever" played under a disco light. Melissa and I slow-danced like wobbling Weebles. She broke the silence.

"Did you do your Latin homework?"

We became friends navigating Mr. Cabico's Filipino accent as he taught us Latin declensions. Melissa tutored me once on how the dative case works.

"I am going to give *you* my pencil," she said. "*You* is the direct object, *pencil* is the dative noun."

I told her no, I did not do my Latin homework, and she frowned and smiled. And just then, just as the Heatwave song climaxed with falsetto singing, just as everyone else started to make out, my gaze moved from Melissa's eyes and down to her big, 36D bazongas pressed up against my stomach.

. . .

Maybe it was the irregular cut of my Marshall's pants. Maybe it was the goldenrod Ambervision hue through which I looked at Melissa in a different light. Whichever the case, I'd avoided looking at Melissa's boobs the whole dance, and what was given to me once I did was a raging, dative-cased, zinc-supplemented boner.

I didn't know one thing about being with another body yet, but I knew what was going on with mine.

. . .

Before we went back to the car, I slipped down the hallway into the school chapel—really a classroom with candles and benches—and entered the confession booth. I never went to confession at my high school, preferring my local parish, except for the one time, the last occasion I took the sacrament, when I had a Vatican II-style, face-to-face repentance of sins senior year with Vice-Principal Father Pete Tarkovsky, at which time I catalogued, among other sins, what I am about to confess to you now. I went into that confession booth, sat on the short bench and, as the muffled strains of Glenn Miller's "In the Mood" cleared out the cafeteria, sat there, and stared at the screen where the priest's face would have been, and prayed down my boner.

It was a holy moment, for lack of a better term. I didn't know a thing about other bodies, but knew this was the only way mine would make it through the evening. After I walked out, I looked up at an unlit crucifix, and I knew I'd remain chaste.

· · ·

Frank and Jimmy drove Melissa and me to Ponzio's Diner to get ice cream. They sat at the bar and drank beers. From their stools, Frank and Jimmy made brumsky-motorboat motions with their hands cupped over imaginary bazongas.

I did not brumsky Melissa's bazongas. I kissed her at the front door, and returned to the backseat. Frank was genuinely pissed. "What kind of a pussy doesn't grab those hooters?"

· · ·

Ten years later, Frank would regard the Philly waterfront runs as too much of a schlep, and after a BJs opened up in Voorhees and Langhorne the door-to-door meatselling business went down the shitter. Jimmy would be discovered by a talent agent and would switch careers from selling real estate in Florida to that of a world-famous Bill Clinton impersonator, who marked up 250 appearances on *The Tonight Show*, countless corporate gigs, and a *Naked Gun* sequel.

But that night, Frank and Jimmy drove the white Cadillac past my house and onto the baseball diamond behind my backyard, into center field. Frank unlocked the doors.

"Get out," Jimmy said. "You can walk home from here."

Frank's Cadillac laid wheels and sprayed my suit with orange infield mud. I hopped over the left field fence, went back to my room, said an "Our Father," and listened to Foreigner on headphones.

45.

Notes on Kerosene

Shortly before he was laid off, Dad bought a blue workout suit from Marshall's. With red piping on the sleeves and sides of the pants, the workout suit looked sharp in an eighties, Run-D.M.C. kind of way, even if he wore leather Jesus sandals and white socks with it. When the suit got nappy, worn down on the elbows and haunches, I realized he had been wearing it for weeks, months on end. In winter, he put a leather jacket over the suit along with a knit cap. He looked like he'd just run out of a house on fire.

• • •

At night I prayed that he would get his job back, get any job, for God to help him even though he didn't believe in Him. Mom broke out her old Merchantville High School cheers. She and Meri took on cleaning projects around the house to keep up morale, washing the bay window's panes until paint chipped off the sill.

"Just because we're poor," Mom announced, "doesn't mean we can't be clean."

• • •

Dad sold off his beloved Dodge Ram pickup. The new owner took off the camper cabin and drove it around town as a beater-upper. Our hearts sank when it passed by, covered in mud. Its replacement, a rusted-out '69 Chevy Impala we got from Grandpop, had a frayed vinyl roof and shot plumes of gray smoke when it idled. When it backfired, which it did often, it sounded like a gunshot.

• • •

I tried my best to lead the life of carefree teenager. Dad would pick me up at the Cherry Hill Mall, and we wouldn't speak. His workout suit grew more frayed and worn.

There was a disconnect between my jaunts to the mall with wads of car wash money and the chronic tensions at home. When the water heater broke, Dad dug into my soapy-wet pockets and took out a weekend's pay to help buy a new boiler. I didn't dare complain.

• • •

For more than a year it went like this. We ate pancakes for dinner, bought generic food at a bulk store called Jewel-T, where customers brought their own boxes, and stocked up on stomach-filling food like corn bread, canned corn, and spaghetti sauce.[9]

• • •

We added another vehicle to our collection: an old Bell Telephone Company van, gutted-out and covered in gray primer. My Uncle Mark got it for $50 and gave it to me for my 15th birthday. After a rear-end collision totaled the Impala, Dad drove the primered van around, the loose gear-shifter held in place with a handkerchief.

---

9 In one draft of this Note, I mentioned we were on welfare, which my mom pounced on. "We were NEVER on welfare," she emailed me. "I just wanted to tell you that. I always worked and owed a chunk to your grandparents, but never did I accept welfare." We did get food stamps, and Mom drove with her dad to Mount Holly to pick them up. "I remember because one time Grandpop had on one black sock and one brown one, and in spite of everything that was so degrading, it made me laugh."

"Financially things are getting very tough," I wrote. "But Dad has a job clinched in a couple months. For Christmas, I only asked for clothes and a small cassette player with headphones for school."

A man with the Charles Dickens-meets-*Gilligan's Island* name of Mr. Thurston E. Boggs approached Dad about starting a new business. Boggs had put together a business plan for a new trucking company called Overland Transport, which would take advantage of new deregulation loopholes. Mr. Boggs, a self-described entrepreneur, hired Dad on the basis of his Mensa membership. Mr. Boggs had failed the test. Dad took us to on a trip to check out his future office, inside a warehouse. We were excited at the thought of Dad having a desk job.

"Grandmom even bought him a plant for his desk," Mom said.

The plan fell through when Mr. Thurston E. Boggs was arrested, and his property repossessed, for financial crimes.

• • •

Things got desperate. I'm still not sure if it was a good or bad thing that our parents did not shield Meri and me from day-to-day money woes. They told us to ignore the bill collection agency calls at dinnertime. To get household items and motor oil, we took up a line of credit at Sears. It was soon frozen and sent to a collection agency.

• • •

Meri remembered how Mom kept up appearances. "The makeup was always on, even before she put on cutoffs on and watered the grass," she told me. "Mom did her hair every morning with hot curlers." She mentions Jean Naté body splash, Jontue perfume, clouds of Final Net hairspray. "She only had two pairs of slacks to wear to work. Mom would iron them every morning and made sure she wore different blouses. I mean, she never let herself go. She'd scoop lipstick out of the tube with her little finger to get a couple more weeks out of it."

. . .

That winter we turned the thermostat down to 50 degrees and planted a kerosene heater in the middle of the living room. It looked like a giant lamp inside a cage, and cranked out enough heat to make the living room toasty.

It was Dad's scheme to save money on heating. We kept a blue barrel of kerosene out in the garage. I would drag the heater out and fill the tank up for the night.

"We used to boil water for tea on it," my mother remembers. "It was like camping out in the living room."

. . .

Light shone through the heater's grate up on the ceiling. It narrowed into a starry circle as the wick ran through the kerosene tank. Every couple hours one of us got out from under the blankets to open the door and let clean air in. Snuffy, our Siberian Husky German Shepherd mix, curled around, dead asleep in doggy bliss.

Out in the garage, kerosene spurted on me as I squeezed the pump into the tank. The smell seeped into my school clothes, shoes, and socks.

46.

Notes on the Moped

"When I turn 16 on February 28, 1983," I wrote to myself, "if I don't have enough money to get a moped, I'll steal one if I have to."

Sweet sixteen came and went. Still no moped.

By May 1983, I had saved $320, enough to buy a Tomos.

Built in Yugoslavia, Tomos mopeds may have been a knockoff brand, but it fit the bill for me. Although I dreamt of doing it, I had never sat on any motorized vehicle until I revved up my new maroon hog that day and sped off the dealer's lot on Route 73.

•   •   •

I'd seen *Quadrophenia* multiple times, and fancied myself a Maple Shade Mod, the Ace Face of Burlington County, minus the interest in ska music and tailored clothes.

At the car wash, I shined up the chrome on the extra mirrors and turn signals I'd bought at Pep Boys. I cruised around South Jersey, my mullet's curls that stuck out beneath my helmet blowing in the wind.

•   •   •

Three weeks later, I cruised into Cherry Hill to visit Paul Stern, a soccer player and all-around good guy. It was Memorial Day weekend. I parked the moped inside their garage, locked the handlebars, and played backyard volleyball with his brothers. I might have been there an hour when I went back inside to check up on my Tomos.

It was gone. Double take. Did you see it? Someone go out for a joy ride?

Nope. It was gone.

. . .

Paul's mom called the Cherry Hill police. A car came, lights off, and the cops asked what kind of moped it was, what color. They circled around the block, behind a nearby strip mall. Nothing. A couple hours later, Dad's rusty Impala backfired up the street. He came out with a tire iron in his hand, ready to drive around and *catch the bastards*. Mr. Stern urged for calm, to wait for the cops to come back. Dad went out on his own.

With each exchange, I felt more embarrassed, for myself, for our junked-up car, for Dad and his ratty clothes. Three years I had saved up for a moped that was stolen in three weeks, but not in Maple Shade, where I was the most cautious, or Camden, where I eyeballed people at red lights, but in fancy-pants Cherry Hill.

. . .

I called in sick from school the rest of the week, watched game shows, and mulled over What This Meant. The loss was obviously more than just a moped. It was also about how a 16-year-old had lost a toy his parents couldn't afford to replace.

"I am the punch line of a cosmic joke," I wrote.

. . .

The reasonable conclusion I came to was that I had been pretending to be someone I wasn't. I had been posing as some preppy Cherry Hill guy, when I was really just a Shader, a guy who works at a car wash and wore off-brand clothes that didn't fit well.

I'm just a poor boy, I thought. *Nobody loves me.*

47.

Notes on "Bohemian Rhapsody"

I was on a TV show, *Sound Affects*. It re-ran for a few months on VH1 late at night. I'd seen flyers that asked people to "share stories of the song that changed your life."

I sent an email about my relationship with a Queen song, "Bohemian Rhapsody." A few days later, I found myself in Fun, a Chinatown nightclub, answering questions posed by a woman with dreadlocks. Growing up in Maple Shade, where everyone listened to AC/DC and drove pickup trucks, I didn't feel like I fit in. Then I heard my first Queen song.

"Before 'Bohemian Rhapsody,'" I said, "my life was in black and white. After that, it was all Technicolor."

◆ ◆ ◆

If someone walked up to me in 1982 and asked me to name my favorite band, I would say, without hesitation, that it was Queen. The Favorite Band Question, for white adolescent males in South Jersey at least, provided a way of finding out what kind of person you were. Were you a metalhead, classic rocker, punker, poseur-punker, Deadhead, Steve Miller Band-preppy? Or maybe you were a Depeche Mode New Waver, or exclusively into Duran Duran, Run-D.M.C., Iron Maiden, Rush? Were you more Madonna or Prince or Springsteen?

These taxonomies mattered. Let me be clear: to say that Queen was my favorite band did not translate as a plus in the social acceptance column.

• ♦ •

For me, Queen was Santa Claus, Jesus, and The Idea of Sex wrapped up in one. I spent nights praying for the chart success of "Radio Ga Ga," Queen's 1984 comeback single. I spent afternoons wondering what the band members thought of while they played their instruments, what John Deacon and Roger Taylor wore when their families skied together in Switzerland. I spent mornings practicing air guitar to Brian May's *Star Fleet* solo EP. And I spent whole weekends listening to Freddie Mercury's voice, eyes closed tight, with a chair jacked up against my bedroom door. Whole days projected onto strangers' faces on album sleeves.

• ♦ •

I'd borrowed a cassette of Queen's *A Night at The Opera* from Andy, a trumpet player in band, when I was nine. My ears had been trained for this moment. As I sat on my room's shag rug and "Bohemian Rhapsody" began, it felt as if small, shiny objects, like atoms or quarks, sprinkled around my ears, then went inside, until, by the gong at the song's finale, it seemed they met in the middle of my head to form a new lobe of my brain.

I rewound the tape and played it again. And again.

• ♦ •

In May 1984, I joined the Official International Queen Fan Club, and shortly thereafter called their London office, using the phone number on *The Works* album sleeve notes. International calling was expensive, but I wanted to talk to someone else—anyone else—who actually liked Queen.

"Hello from America!" I announced. "Had the boys been around today? Have you seen them?"

"No, not today," the fan club guy said. "They're out on tour."

Of course, I said to myself. *Didn't you know that?*

140

I struggled to think of anything else to say. "It would be nice to live in England, where there are more Queen fans."

"Well," the fan club guy said, "we did have another person from America who sent their membership form in."

"Really? Who?"

My mind raced. Maybe this person lives nearby? If not, we could be pen pals? Or maybe this person was a girl, a pretty one?

"Yes, let's see," he said, flipping papers. "That person...is...you."

I don't think I've ever felt so alone.

48.

Notes on Main Street Music

When a *Maple Shade Progress* story announced that a record store was opening in town, I just about crapped my pants. Reading this piece of news was like hearing the Dork Cavalry was riding to town to save us. Instead of feigning interest at baseball games at friends' houses, I could flip through records all day!

"The boy that rides his hobby gently," Ralph Waldo Emerson wrote in his journal, "must always give way to the boy that rides his hobby hard." My hobby was collecting records. And this dork rode his hobby hard.

. . .

I studied up on Frankie Marsden, the store's owner. I wanted to make sure he would like me and would let me hang out for hours on end. A soccer coach who worked as a substitute teacher at Maple Shade High School in the early 1970s—my Aunt Chrissy remembers him as "the nice guy who let us talk in study hall"—Frankie managed Sound Odyssey, a record store in the Cherry Hill Mall that was dimly lit and had walls lined with red shag carpeting, like interior of a 70s van with bubble windows. It was Frankie's dream to run his own store in Maple Shade.

Frankie transplanted everything you'd see in a mall record store in the 1980s: a Top 40 singles rack, a new releases timeline on a chalkboard, a floor display panel filled with bikini car wash and black-light Led Zeppelin posters. Main Street Music's glass storefront was covered with record covers and cardboard cutouts. A tape rack from a closed Sound Odyssey filled one wall of the store. The used records came from Frankie's own collection at first, but soon people brought in their own LPs to trade for new music and these new things called compact discs.

. . .

Frankie wore metal-framed glasses and had a bald head ringed with unruly curls. Everything Frankie played in the store was listenable in a knockoff Beatles way. Whenever he grooved to a song on the turntable, he'd sway his torso left to right, Ringo Starr-style, totaling up a customer's purchase with one arm and holding the LP up with the other. I recall listening to Fairport Convention, Renaissance, Shoes, Raspberries, the first Bangles album. His favorite records were by the Strawbs, a progressive folk outfit from England with a logo that looked like a roadside steak house's, all serifs and lines, like a Wild West wanted poster.

. . .

Along with the car wash job, hanging out at Main Street Music replaced sports, clubs, the school newspaper—every extracurricular activity. I got off the bus, and instead of walking down Coles Avenue to my house, I went straight down Main Street, still in dress pants and a Chess King leather tie, and hung out with my fellow Shader Record Nerds.

Main Street Music was an alternate universe where the things I cared about not only were recognized but mattered. Old dudes with dyed-black hair and a *Record Collector* under their arms flipped through stacks. If someone came to sell off a collection, we'd lurk by the register to get first dibs as Frankie priced them.

• • •

Frankie wrote record reviews for the *Burlington County Times*, which I saw as the apex of what one could do with one's life. To get paid to write about music? And get free records? Never mind he got paid just twenty bucks for each article, or that he picked Whitney Houston's self-titled debut as the best album of 1984. Frankie wrote things about music and then people read those things. He even had an author photo. He taped his clips on the counter, and I told him how I agreed with him or thought he was full of shit. The best part was that he listened.

• • •

Frankie never seemed to mind I stayed there for hours on end, along with Jim, the Iron Maiden fan with a secret love for Linda Ronstadt, and Andy, the trumpet player who knew everything about The Who. Maybe he let me stay for the same reason restaurants seat you by the window, so people believe there are plenty of customers inside. Maybe Frankie was afraid of telling me to leave. I just know he just never turned me away.

49.

Notes on Day 90

Mike Nester got the elusive call number 30, right on Day 90. He clocked in, didn't say anything, finished his shift, and filed union papers the next morning. The company said they made a mistake, but after he appealed to the Teamsters Local, Dad was back on the rolls. I was a high school junior and could barely remember the last time my father held a regular job.

As he prepared to return to work, Dad went on a shopping spree: new work clothes, a leather jacket, and a pair of $80 steel-toed work boots. He shed his unemployment weight, put in loads of overtime, and came home at 3 a.m., 4 a.m., sometimes when the sun came up.

His car would sometimes pass me as I walked to the bus stop at 6:30 a.m.

. . .

Mom began to ask about paychecks. He wasn't passing them over to pay the bills. He handed over cash instead. Not even pay-stubs: he kept those in his locked briefcase.

Dad's new manner was mysterious, even more distant, un-recognizable; Mom's naïveté, too, was unrecognizable.

Maybe, Mom reasoned, Dad was still depressed. Or he wanted to move—which my mother described as a "constant, absolutely constant" request. I thought that desire had subsided while he was out of work. It had only intensified.

"I was afraid he was going to just pluck us up and move us someplace," my mother said.

That place had been Arizona for years. Just when Mom was going to give in, he switched it up. "Well, how about Montana?" he asked.

· · ·

"I could tell something was up," is how she puts it now. "I just thought he was having a mental problem." One morning, after the kids went to school and Dad not yet home, Mom sat at the dining room table and wrote a letter to her husband.

What's wrong?
What's the matter?
I know something is troubling you.
I know something is bothering you.
What can I do?
How can I help you?
Let's talk.

Notes on Confession

Mom sat Meri and me on her bed. It was the day before Thanksgiving. She smoothed down the bedspread before we flopped on it. We could see she'd been crying. The shades were drawn shut.

"Your father is having an affair," Mom began. "He confessed to it today. He has a girlfriend, a younger woman. He's had one for a while." There was the slightest pause. "And he's been having," deep breath, pause, "sex with her."

She didn't know what was going to happen, other than that we had to stay at Grandmom and Grandpop's for a couple days.

End of meeting.

◆　◆　◆

Meri and I kept our eyes down as we walked into her room.

"What's going to happen?" she asked. "Are they going to get *divorced*?"

Meri was the tough sibling, tougher than me. She never let on what she felt. As she sobbed on her four-poster bed with pink drapes, I was reminded that Meri was my little sister. We had been told the adult version of what was happening.

For once, I didn't cry. And I didn't have a clue what to tell her.

51.

Notes on a Truck Driver Separation

There is no two-house solution in a truck driver separation. There's a house and a motel.

◆　◆　◆

After Dad confessed to the affair and before Mom called us into their bedroom, she had booted him out of the house.

◆　◆　◆

We didn't own luggage, so we stuffed our clothes into trash bags and brought them to our grandparents. Mom spent three afternoons on her parents' bed. Surrounded by her sisters and her mother, covered in blankets, Mom laid there in shock, her body cold. Aunt Terry put heating pads on her feet. Aunt Chrissy patted down her forehead.

◆　◆　◆

Mom went back to the house one day to find a bouquet of roses in the bedroom with a note attached.
I love you, I have always loved you, and I will always love you.
I'm sorry.
Mom tore the note into little pieces and threw the roses across the lawn. Another day I came back from school and the backyard was dotted with swatches of shiny fabric. Mom had taken out of the closet every nightgown, every piece of underwear—"every piece of clothing that I wore to try to look nice for him," she

said—and, with a pair of scissors, systematically cut each garment into small pieces. She then threw them out the back window.

. . .

Thirty years later, my wife and I were getting rid of baby clothes, and it made me unbearably anxious. I realized that it was the plop of those little shirts and pants, and the subsequent crinkle of the trash bags, that reminded me of those days packing up to leave the house. It reminded me of the first time I saw my parents not as giants or ambassadors of God, but as fallible, failing adults.

52.

Notes on My First Girlfriend

I went to Main Street Music to buy records and get out of the house. But I also met my first girlfriend there.

Kathy Lively was her name. Everything I am about to describe regarding Kathy Lively and our relationship will sound wholesome, and that's because it was.

• • •

I spotted Kathy Lively one morning at mass. She had blonde Princess Diana hair. After mass, I went down to Main Street Music to check out the new batch of 45 singles. And there was the same girl—same Princess Diana hair, same teal-blue skirt and white tuxedo shirt. She stood at the counter checking out a Cure cassette. (I know this because I checked on what she bought with Frankie.) I summoned the courage to say hello and asked if I could walk her home, which happened to be right down the street.

"I guess so," she said. That's pretty much all she ever said to me.

• • •

Kathy Lively belonged to the rarest of all species in my hometown, the equivalent of a Northern Spotted Owl: a Shader girl who loved Duran Duran and The Smiths and dressed cool.

• • •

As far as I could tell, Kathy Lively dated me for the following two reasons: first, I lived nearby, and so wouldn't mind hanging out in her house watching MTV, which was all we did; and second, in the rarest moments of letting her guard down, Kathy told me she thought I resembled Limahl, the lead singer of Kajagoogoo.

. . .

I'd get off the bus and walk a half block to her house and watch Martha Quinn and Alan Hunter for hours in their living room on a couch covered in soft cotton sheets. Her mom brought out, I shit you not, trays of juice and cookies. Her dad, whom I never saw, drove an armored truck. She and her younger sister, McKenzee, wore Molly Ringwald dresses and didn't speak to anyone else in town. McKenzee poked fun at me whenever I tried to hold Kathy's hand. When I left, we made out for three minutes by the gate. "Can I see you again?" I asked.

"I guess so," she said.

. . .

Then I fucked up. That summer, I made out with a Canadian girl under the Wildwood boardwalk. She spoke French and wore a half-shirt. After that I suspected there were greener, sluttier pastures out there to be explored. My hookup weighed down on me: I had cheated on my first girlfriend, which seemed significant in a house living under the weight of adultery. Out of guilt, I asked Kathy if we could take a break.

"I guess so," she said.

A single tear went down her face. It was the only indication she had any emotional investment in our relationship. And in that moment, I realized what I had done was cruel and foolish.

Any currency I had as a fan of Oingo Boingo and Black Flag didn't go very far with girls at Camden Catholic. The better part of my sophomore year was taken up by attempts to look more and more Limahl-like to win Kathy Lively back. I cut off the sleeves of all my t-shirts. I grew out my new wave mullet, died it yellow with lemon juice. I wore straw hats. I put on lip gloss. None of these Limahl-ifying efforts had any effect on Kathy Lively. I begged her on a weekly basis to take me back. Each time Kathy Lively said no.

• • •

This first heartbreak, self-inflicted, led to my purchase of, among other I-want-you-back schlock, John Waite's "Missing You," Paul Young's "Every Time You Go Away," and Phil Collins's "Against All Odds (Take a Look at Me Now)." I stacked these 45s on Main Street Music's counter with my head bowed the way fallen men order drinks at dives. At home I sang along, alone.

Notes on a Town Called Malice

West Woodlawn Avenue curves around the Shitty-Go-Round sewage processing plant and continues up as Park Avenue. This was where Scot Harter lived.

• ◆ •

Scot Harter struck boys out in CYO with a wicked sideways Gene Garber wind-up. I first met him at The Great Maple Shade Rock Fight of 1979. Kids from our side of the Shitty-Go-Round defended a construction site's hill of rocks from the boys of Roland Avenue. Scot and his friends, all three years older than me, conscripted boys to set up a Maginot Line of plywood around the hill. When the boys from Roland Avenue—men-children all, with premature mustaches and surrounded by Pigpen dirt clouds—charged the hill in a scene straight out of *Jason and the Argonauts*, Scot and his friends hightailed it home. The Roland Avenue boys took me prisoner, threw rocks at my feet until I escaped and ran home.

• ◆ •

Cut to May 1984. I am walking up to the Hilltop Deli to play Defender, and pass Scot's pink rancher. I admired his gunmetal-blue Chevy Nova parked in his driveway. Scot came up to his screen door.

"Yo, Nester. I hear you're into music."

I was surprised he knew my name. "Yeah, sure," I said. "I've got 250 records and 100 tapes. I haven't counted my 45s."

Such a catalogue must have made Scot smile. Sure, you have a collection. But what's *actually in* your collection?

"You into punk rock at all?"[10]

"Sure. I got Ramones albums," I said. "My favorite new band now is R.E.M."

Scot paused a second. "They're all right," he said. "But they're too commercial."

Too commercial? R.E.M. had only put out two albums, and they'd sold out already? Scot went back indoors, and brought out a short stack of LPs, all in pristine condition. As I flipped through the covers, I recognized some from *Record*, *Musician*, *The Bob*, and other music rags I read.

"Why don't you borrow these and let me know what you think?"

• • •

If I could point to one moment when I was assured there was a way out of Maple Shade, where I could say there is a Before and an After, where someone or some force interceded and changed the way I looked at the world, one example would be when Scot Harter handed to 13-year-old me Hüsker Dü's *Zen Arcade*,

---

10 This exchange sounds staged now. Who isn't *into punk rock*? But to pose such a question in Maple Shade, which just turned Reagan Democrat, where FM rock issued out of every bitchin' Camaro or F150, where no one would predict they'd all be listening to country in 30 years, was like asking if you read communist literature in the 1950s. The stilted and dated dialogue, reproduced here, sounds straight out of a coming-of-age movie: the slightly older docent takes the greenhorn under his wing, down the path of codependency and reefer madness. But that's how I remember it, and there's no way to make it cooler or dress it up as more sophisticated. Did there come a moment when I stepped back and said to myself, *Self, you are listening to some really dorky music, this Phil Collins and Billy Joel and Linda Ronstadt, and a lot of it's just plain shitty*? No. Please keep in mind that in 1984 the CBGB's scene wasn't exactly knocking down doors in The Shade. Taste moved in increments for Catholic boys in the suburbs.

The Replacements' *Tim*, Stiff Little Fingers' *Inflammable Material*, the first Bad Brains LP, *Another Music in a Different Kitchen* by the Buzzcocks, Wire's *Pink Flag*, and *Snap!*, a greatest hits collection by Scot's favorite band and soon to be one of mine, The Jam.

• • •

I turned around and went back to my room and turntable. I would never play Defender with Shader stoners again. I would suspend listenings of Foreigner and Billy Joel. Some of these records got played so much over the course of the next two weeks that I had Frankie order Scot replacements. And then I wore them out again.

54.

Notes on the Sharon Motor Inn

I was wrong about what I said before, that there is no two-house solution in a truck driver separation. There's no motel. There's just a house and a couch.

. . .

After a week, Mom called Dad at the Sharon Motor Inn on Route 73, a mile away from the bar where Martin Luther King, Jr. was thrown out and four blocks away from the Mallard Inn, where I was conceived.[11]

"We don't have enough money for you to stay there," she said. "You have to come home."

Dad slept on the couch. He tried to get back into the bedroom, and a couple nights, through the walls, I heard Mom's wallop-slaps on his chest, then sobs. *How could you do this?* I heard over and over.

I put my headphones on and turned the volume up. Way up.

. . .

Dad wanted to stay. For his creature comforts, if not for anything else, Mom said: the bookshelf, his chair, the house to himself all day before he went out to work.

---

11 "Take time to play," reads a Mallard Inn matchbook I recently bought online. "It is the secret of perpetual youth."

One morning, he fell asleep on my sister's bed, and my mother went berserk, grabbed him, and pulled him off the pink sheets, half asleep, pushed him onto the floor.

. . .

I never knew who the other woman was. I didn't even know her name. I know now.

. . .

Leanne S., a younger woman from Mount Holly, worked in the office, called the "truck barn." She had a newborn baby and lived with a long-haul trucker who was not the father. At 26, she was 11 years younger than my mother.

"Of course he wasn't working overtime all those nights," my mother said. "He was screwing around with the girl at work."

My mother has grown much tougher and much less naïve over the years, and much more plainspoken. I never would have heard her say "screwing" growing up.

. . .

I developed a theory about my father's miraculous call number 30. I asked my mother over the phone one time.

"Do you think Leanne made the thirtieth call happen? I mean, it was such a fluke thing that he got the thirtieth call and made the rolls, and over other guys with more seniority. Do you think Leanne had anything to do with it, working in the truck barn and all?"

Mom thought a second. She took a drag from cigarette. "I don't know," she said. "All I know is that she was a dumb old sleazy whore."

• • •

"Look at it as a man," my Aunt Chrissy said to me. "He's out of work, gaining weight, he's on high-blood-pressure medication—that affects your sexuality. He's probably depressed, maybe even impotent."

"Then he finally gets back his job, his dignity. And somebody pays a little bit of attention to him in a positive way, this woman at his work, and something inside him says, *Maybe I am OK.* You would have to be a saint."

"Listen: what he did was inexcusable," she said, "but that doesn't mean that he didn't love your mother. It doesn't mean he didn't love you or your sister. The man may have had his own freaking breakdown."

• • •

I didn't talk to Dad for months. Whenever he and I were in the house, I made my silence conspicuous. I walked past him into my room, blasted the stereo, lifted weights, slammed dumbbells down on the floor.

One day, Mom knocked on the door. "Your father wants to talk to you," she said.

Dad and I climbed into the gray-primered van, its engine humming and heating up between the two front seats, and drove up and down Main Street.

"I didn't mean to hurt your mother," he said. "What happened with that woman, it was all about pussy. It didn't mean a thing."

• • •

My head jerked back. I fixed my gaze ahead, toward the road. I'd never heard him say *pussy* before. Dad never cursed at all, except for one time when I was about nine. He had the station wagon on ramps and was changing the oil. He hadn't let the motor cool

158

down enough, and so when he unscrewed the manifold bolt, out poured hot oil on his hands.

"Fuck! Motherfucker! Fuck!" he screamed. I rolled around on the grass, laughing.

Five years later he's saying *pussy* in the primered van. Other than the *Playboys* and *Penthouses* I kept out in the woods, I had never even seen a pussy.

. . .

How did I respond? Did he ask to be forgiven? Did he say, *I'm seeing the same thing you're seeing,* or ask me how I justified my presence in the universe?

. . .

Before we went back inside, he stashed an item in his briefcase. He always kept it next to him. This time, however, he left his briefcase open on his seat. Maybe he was rattled after talking about pussy with his son, but I never saw that briefcase open or unlocked. There, on top of a pile of papers, was a small datebook, with a note to himself from September 1983:

Patti found out about Leanne. Damn.

55.

Notes on Juvenile Delinquency, in the Second Person

Jaguars are welded to the hood. For Mercedes, you need a band saw. The wire goes down into the block and makes a big twang sound when you cut it free. Chrysler zirconia pentagrams aren't even worth your time, but you'd need wire cutters or a duckbill lock breaker for it.

· · ·

You learned all this through trial and bloody-handed error, bored from taking so many Cadillac ornaments off hoods. Caddy ornaments are the easiest to rip off. You could spot a coat of arms from a block away, your eyes trained from watching them fall off hoods at the car wash.

· · ·

Around 15, you began to wonder why the world didn't pluck you out of obscurity. You thought taking a bus out of town in a tie each day would help, but all you ended up doing was going back home to buy records and drink beer in the woods.

· · ·

You spend days at the car wash and watched yuppies knock on the glass from inside their windshields, pointing at some speck of bugshit or load of tree sap bonded to the glass. Anything that stuck out of a car chassis gave you grief. Whenever some polo shirt dude drove off the track and complained how their Cadillac emblem had been felled by brushes, you resisted saying *what did you think would happen?* You gave him a free wash.

• • •

You biked through Cherry Hill, fucked-up on whatever flavor Mad Dog an old man got you from the liquor store, and took out your anger on Cadillac emblems.

You went for the new and shiny ones first. You threw your bike into a bush in case you had to make a getaway by foot. You walked beside a Caddy, took in the new car smell, and dragged your fingers over the paint. Then you put your right foot up on the bumper, cupped the emblem in a reverse reacharound, and yanked straight up.

All that kept a Caddy emblem in place was a thick paperclip that made a tinkle sound when you pulled it off. If you tipped it *just so*, it made no sound at all. You never got caught never got caught never got caught.

• • •

You wanted the citizens of Cherry Hill to have their toys stolen. As you biked home, two or three Caddy emblems in each pocket sticking into your thighs, you pulled up to a Caddy in The Shade and put one on the hood, like you're the Cadillac Emblem Robin Hood or something.

As you sobered up and watched David Letterman, you dared your father to come home.

Notes on the Junior Prom,
Joni Mitchell, and My Deflowering

Friday, April 19, 1985. The night of my junior prom. After asking out a succession of Cherry Hill girls—Stacey, Denise, Jackie, Angela—and having been rejected by all of them, I stayed home. Back home, Dad returned to his mysterious overtime routines. Mom went to grandmom's to deal with some sister-marriage drama. And Meri was out on one of her many dates.

◆ ◆ ◆

The house empty, I lit candles on the coffee table, sat in the middle of the living room, drank a bottle of homemade raisin wine stolen from the basement, and listened to Joni Mitchell, from her late folk to early jazz periods: *Blue, For the Roses, Court and Spark, Hissing of Summer Lawns, Hejira.* I cried. I wailed. I convulsed. I flipped the tapes over and cried some more.

◆ ◆ ◆

We both know, dear reader, that this is yet another example of how the present moment assigns mythic importance to something from the past. I honestly do remember thinking of that night of crying and singing and candles as a Turning Point. I had to assign a badge to myself for each experience, which I saw as another step on the road to discovering myself.

That was the night I earned the Crying All Night to Joni Mitchell Badge.

Saturday, April 20, 1985. The night I lost my virginity. By this point I was hanging out equally with Shaders and Camden Catholic kids, and since everyone was partied out from the prom, I decided to make like my sister and head up to the Wawa to see what was happening. I got into a car with some Shader dude whose name I forget. He picked up his girlfriend, whose name I forget. We drank Jack Daniel's in the back of a store, the location of which I forget. Then went back to my house, and I had sex with the girlfriend's friend, whose name I forget.

. . .

She walked in, took a swig of Jack. We made out and then we did it. It was a rushed, clumsy affair—doggy style on the rug, pants still half on—and we didn't finish. It was, strictly speaking, a few thrusts. My sister walked in on us, and we put our pants back on. The Shader dude kept banging his girlfriend in my bed, finished, then took off, and that was end of that.

. . .

It didn't really bother me that I forgot my deflowerer's name until I told people later on. "How could you be so crass?" they asked. Factor in that I knew that the girl with whom I shared this tryst was *experienced* (aka *wasn't a virgin*, aka *was considered easy*) and there's some potential for judgment or self-slut-shaming (all of which I want to avoid). All these years I've believed the fact that my deflowering occurred 24 hours after spending the night with Joni Mitchell tapes was the most special part of the story. The girl was incidental.

• • •

My sister has a photographic memory. This conversation took place on America Online Instant Messenger in August 2006.

MeriMumzie (my sister): You rang??

Murlinson (me): hey. I have to ask you couple questions.

MeriMumzie: absolutely. shoot em off

Murlinson: Think back to 1985.

MeriMumzie: k...Hair=brownish, braces=final year

Murlinson: Who was that vaguely guido guy from Shade I was hanging with?

MeriMumzie: Hmmm, Joe Spiotti?

Murlinson: Sounds close, but no -- he was in your class.

MeriMumzie: Don DiCallo?

Murlinson: Nope. You know, string mustache, fancied himself a ladies' man.

MeriMumzie: I am thinking.

Murlinson: We brought girls back to our house one night.

MeriMumzie: Not Bobby Roberts who I worked with at Kinney... is it?

Murlinson: YES!!!! Do you remember the night we brought girls back to the house?

MeriMumzie: Yep.

Murlinson: Um, It was the night I lost my virginity.

MeriMumzie: Barf!

Murlinson: She was the sister of some guy who was older than us.

MeriMumzie: Debbie [Name Redacted], younger sister of Shawn [Name Redacted]

Murlinson: Oh my god — you remember her name?

MeriMumzie: She was a ho bag extraordinaire... Short black hair, bulby nose, brown eyes, skinny-ish...tight jeans, striped shirt...hoodie jacket

Murlinson: Oh my god.

MeriMumzie: I dont have a problem with remembering outfits and hair styles.

Murlinson: You actually remember what she wore that night?

MeriMumzie: Yeah, tight, slightly faded Jordache jeans, comb in pocket, and a grey and navy striped (horizontal) striped ballet shirt and those white roach killer "jazz shoes" that tied.

Murlinson: This is fucking freaky.

MeriMumzie: Frightening, I know.

Murlinson: I am writing about this night, because it was the night after my junior prom at Camden Catholic, which I did not attend. I stayed home and cried to Joni Mitchell.

MeriMumzie: Why are you going there dude??

57.

Notes on Shader Record Nerds: A Manifesto

If you talked to me then, you would encounter an unremarkable specimen of adolescent malaise; you'd also find someone ready to explain the world through his sensibility, which we will call the Shader Record Nerd Sensibility.

· · ·

Shader Record Nerds read *Aquarian Weekly*, *The Bob*, *Record*, *New York Rocker*, *Rolling Stone*. They made lists of bands and memorized them.

· · ·

Shader Records Nerds were what we would now call "mansplainers." To the Shader Record Nerd, musical taste directly reflected someone's personal judgment. If *Led Zeppelin II* or the *Steve Miller Band's Greatest Hits* were permanent fixtures in your car's cassette deck, you weren't just lame; you demonstrated an aggressive lack of taste.

· · ·

Shader Record Nerds accredited themselves through a years-long process.

Shader Record Nerds were annoying to most people other than other Shader Record Nerds.

. . .

"Every human being has his shell," Madame Merle says to Isabel in Henry James's *The Portrait of a Lady*. "You must take the shell into account." Shader Record Nerds adjudicated others' shells by looking through someone's record collection at a party. If they spotted a Billy Ocean or Kenny Loggins LP, that person's shell was determined to be lame.

. . .

Shader Record Nerds know their folklore: that it's Doug Yule who sings lead vocals on "Candy Says," not Lou Reed; that Dweezil Zappa played the solo on the latest Don Johnson single.

Shader Record Nerds know that, if you listen closely, you can hear Mick Jagger singing with Carly Simon on "You're So Vain." Shader Record Nerds will be first to tell you it was Clover, Huey Lewis's old band, that backs up Elvis Costello on *My Aim Is True*, not The Attractions.

Shader Record Nerds don't need to be told Judas Priest's "Diamonds and Rust" is, in fact, a Joan Baez cover.

. . .

In case it isn't obvious already, Shader Record Nerds were mostly dudes. At least on paper, most Shader Record Nerds were heterosexual but were most likely virgins. Their very presence repelled all women and girls. Shader Record Nerds liked to brag about their Canadian girlfriends, Europe trip dalliances with British girls who liked music, and hot second cousins who lived out of state.

. . .

Shader Record Nerds studied every music-related urban myth. Play a Zeppelin, Queen, or Styx record backward and you will turn into, respectively, a Satanist, homo, or pothead. Paul McCartney died in 1966 and was replaced by a lookalike. Jim Morrison was alive and living in rural Oregon. Ozzy Osbourne bit off a bird's head at every concert as Satanist sacrifice. Rod Stewart was put in the hospital to have his stomach pumped for drinking a gallon of semen. Gene Simmons's tongue was once a horse's, surgically transplanted into his mouth.

· · ·

Shader Record Nerds knew all these stories were false but knew that myths always had the last word.

· · ·

Perhaps the apotheosis of Shader Record Nerd Folklore involves the 1992 death of Toto drummer Jeff Porcaro, whose allergic reaction to pesticide while working in his yard, along with the long-term effects of cocaine use, led to massive heart failure. This story, an example of real life imitating art, gave the Shader Record Nerd the chance to explain with a straight face that there was once a drummer who did in fact die in a "bizarre gardening accident," as prophesied in the 1982 mockumentary *This Is Spinal Tap*, in which band member David St. Hubbins explains that former Tap drummer John "Stumpy" Pepys met the same horticulturally induced end. The Porcaro Story offers an excuse for the Shader Record Nerd to rattle off more quotes from the movie, which is part of a behavior we might call Shader Record Nerd Tourette's, and an excuse to review Jeff Porcaro's non-Toto, 20-year legacy as a session drummer on records from Seals & Crofts to Michael Jackson's *Thriller*.

Shader Record Nerds drove down Main Street, around South Jersey and Philly, on the way to Third Street Jazz and Philly Record Exchange, and wrestled for control of the cassette deck: late Talk Talk, new Replacements, LL Cool J, early Prince, jazz-period Joni Mitchell with Jaco Pastorious, That Petrol Emotion, Kate Bush, Aztec Camera.

. . .

The epistemology of the Shader Record Nerd: to collect is to know.

. . .

Shader Record Nerds believed in virtuosity. Precision. Competence. Little Matthew Arnolds in training, Shader Record Nerds held back any abandon or rebellion in favor of an argument over the "10 Most Proficient Metal Bass Players" or "5 Best Piano Players in Rock." Music had to be crafted. Exact. Maple Shade wasn't a Germs or Shaggs town. No room for Outsider Art or sincere hobbyists. Shader Record Nerds believed you were either in the canon or out of the canon, you either rocked or did not rock.

58.

Notes on Negative Capability, R.E.M., and Piscataway

John Keats, in a letter to his brothers George and Thomas, defined the term "negative capability" as "when man is capable of being in uncertainties, mysteries, doubts without any irritable reaching after fact and reason." Keats, talking about Shakespeare, couldn't quite explain any other way how his characters existed without agency.

· · ·

I love the term "negative capability" even though I'm not sure what it means. I love that I both understand the term and don't, which is what the term is all about. Or at least that's what I think it means. "We hate poetry that has a palpable design on us," Keats writes. I think about that when I try to describe my love of R.E.M. as a teenager.

· · ·

Keats again: "Let us not therefore go hurrying about and collecting honey, bee-like buzzing here and there impatiently from a knowledge of what is to be aimed at; but let us open our leaves like a flower and be passive and receptive—budding patiently under the eye of Apollo and taking hints from every noble insect that favours us with a visit."

· · ·

For years I'd been collecting honey without tasting it, filling shelves with records without thinking of it as music first, object second. For years I'd had "diligent indolence" without "wise passiveness."

· · ·

I couldn't understand a fucking word Michael Stipe sang. No one could. I didn't want to understand, or I didn't mind not knowing. *Musician* magazine told me to buy their records and so I did: I got *Reckoning* first, then *Murmur*. Scot had their first EP, *Chronic Town*, on vinyl. The R.E.M. I speak of here—the first four albums—had no palpable design. Michael Stipe sang but did not make sense, and that's why I loved R.E.M. Their music didn't reach for fact or reason. It was the sound of words that weren't words. I sang along phonetically, the way girls do, the way poseurs do, the way losers do. And for once, I didn't care. Until R.E.M., to know and love was to collect. R.E.M. was all about the reaching.

· · ·

The October 1984 issue of *Record* magazine featured an article by R.E.M. guitarist Peter Buck titled "The True Spirit of American Rock." R.E.M. didn't want for press around this time—there were reviews and profiles in just about every issue of every rock magazine. This article was different. It was written by someone *from* R.E.M., and he was talking about what mattered to *him* about music, which he called "the alternative scene."

"Music simply doesn't mean that much to most of the people who buy records," Buck wrote. "I'm 27 and I own one piece of furniture, a ratty old couch given to me out of pity by R.E.M.'s manager, Jefferson Holt. I'm sure there are people who'd be shocked by the way I live, just as I'm shocked when I go to someone's house and see nothing but John Denver, Barry Manilow, and Chicago records. How could they listen to that? Well they *don't*. That's their version of my crummy couch."

Along with providing a list of bands to check out for my next trips to the record store—The dB's, Minutemen, Mission of Burma, others—Buck's article helped me adopt a live-and-let-live credo about non-record nerds, to be content with being "moved by music made by real people for real reasons."

◆ ◆ ◆

Unlike Queen or The Jam or other new wave bands I glommed onto and collected, R.E.M. was playing concerts, and so, the weekend after my deflowering, Scot Harter and I drove up to Rutgers University to see them play a free outdoor show. He picked me up in his flashy car, and we listened to punk and New Wave bands—with exotic names like XTC, Style Council, Red Guitars, The Smiths, Undertones—all the way up the Turnpike.

Around Exit 8, Scot produced a bottle of Hiram Walker peach schnapps from his glove compartment.

"Do you know what this is good for?" he said, opening the bottle, holding up the cap in his left hand. Before I could answer, he rolled down the window and threw the schnapps cap out onto the Turnpike. "Absolutely nothing!"

We passed the schnapps bottle back and forth on the road to Piscataway. When we got there we drank bottles of Hacker-Schoor Oktobkerfest. I was already blotto by the time R.E.M. took the stage.

◆ ◆ ◆

About fifty people swayed on the wet, muddy grass beside a quad. I looked around at the college kids: Goths in white makeup and long black coats, others with moppy hair and flannel shirts.

They all drank cases of Red White & Blue beer. The prim Camden Catholic girls always looked made-up. The girls at the R.E.M. concert wore sundresses and big boots and had long, unteased hair. And they danced. Here, it looked as if no one cared how they looked. I now know this isn't the case—New Wave and punk kids were just as constructed as the Madonna wannabes and the Dance Party USA line dancers—but what was important was the point, then fairly new, of trying to look as if one didn't care how they looked. As someone who wore a necktie to school, this notion, *taking hints from every noble insect,* was shocking.

· · ·

I arrived at the show wearing white jeans, untied Docksides, and a poncho with a Corona beer logo on it. I threw the poncho away in a trashcan, cut off my jeans with a pocketknife, and put on a *Murmur* t-shirt.

· · ·

Oh yeah, the concert. It was great. R.E.M. had two and a half records out by then, and played stuff from their new album, *Fables of the Reconstruction.* Another lesson learned on that muddy field: it's not necessary to recognize every song a band plays, or to have encyclopedic knowledge of what is in front of you. You can just enjoy it. It's possible to simply experience an event without collecting it.

"Could everyone turn around and look at the sunset?" Michael Stipe asked before the encore. "It's so beautiful."

Fifty New Wavers shifted their feet in the soft ground. The already-empurpled sky darkened more, and the band started another song, which I didn't recognize at first. Then Stipe started singing. "Someone told me long ago/there's a calm before the storm."

It was the only words he sang that I understood. It was a cover of Credence Clearwater Revival's "Have You Ever Seen the Rain?" It was played a million times on classic rock radio, along with every other old song stations insisted on playing instead of anything new. This time, standing there in the mud with a new T-shirt and a six-pack of beer in my stomach, something old was new again.

. ⋅ .

The sun set at 7:51 p.m. in Piscataway, N.J. that night.

Notes on Heads

To weigh a human head still attached to a living body, you must lower yourself slowly onto a scale while hanging upside down. The instant the vertebrae start moving toward the skull, you stop and read the scale. Because your neck is not imparting any force onto your head, this isolates your head from your neck.

· · ·

Every Thanksgiving, each member of my family weighed their heads. This tradition began in 1984. Amid casserole dishes, the side plates of small pickles, cans of beer in the living room, uncles busting my balls, we weighed our heads.

· · ·

The paterfamilias, Daniel Curtis Little, who saved the world from kamikazes, had just retired. He spent his golden years weighing filets on a scale for Uncle Frank's meat business. On Thanksgiving, his scale rested on the sideboard, and Grandmom adorned it like a centerpiece with dried flowers and shellacked gourds.

Once everyone had enough Schlitz in them, someone lifted Meri into the air, such that only the side of her skull rested on the stainless steel flatbed. Someone wrote our head weights on a Turnpike card. I recall the coldness of the plate against my ear that first time. My own head has consistently weighed just over 9.5 pounds, or approximately 20 cuts of filet mignon.

．　．　．

In a photo from a Thanksgiving at my grandparents' house, Mike Nester looks away from the camera. His right hand holds a cigarette about to ash in an empty can, his left encircles a Jack and Coke. He sits on the couch in the far corner, his eyes dull and lifeless, pointed at the TV.

He would wait for an elderly woman to appear onscreen, or a black person, or someone in a wheelchair, or anyone else on his tediously long shit list of unacceptables and inferiors, and he would pull out an imaginary pistol from an imaginary holster, and aim at the screen. He would then put one arm under the other in a Weaver stance.

Chick-Chick!

He pauses, aims.

Boom!

This doesn't make people laugh. We just ignore him.

Notes on Getting Arrested

Why I was invited to a keg party down the shore, and by a cheerleader at that, I still don't know. But I went. We were all going to be seniors, after all, and down the shore, subdivisions in the high school halls and shopping malls seemed to matter less. The party was in the older part of Ocean City, the opposite end of the island from where my family stayed. This was the old money end.

. . .

A couple girls rented the house under their parents' names. Jocks in polos with upturned collars or half shirts stood by cases of cheap beer stacked in the hallway, bottles of vodka in the freezer, a bathtub full of ice. One of the jocks was Kurt Youngblood, the bully from OLPH, who went to Camden Catholic and became a big football player. For years, if Kurt came near me in the hallways, I ducked out of the way or put my head inside my locker. And here I was on my knees in front of him in a shore house kitchen, as he and his friends set up a beer bong—two Bud tallboys poured down a funnel and force-drunk from a tube. Kurt pushed my shoulders down with one hand, stuck the tube in my mouth with the other, and I held on as they lifted the funnel.

I gagged, spit out on the floor. Then I drank another. And another.

. . .

A couple hours later I wobbled down the boardwalk with some football players looking for funnel cake. Everything was closed. Someone decided to take out his frustration on Junior's Miniature Golf Course, which had left open its gate. The other goons walked right in.

"Stay here," one of them said. "Stand lookout."

I swayed in the middle of the boardwalk, took in the sound of the waves and the sea air, and watched Camden Catholic's offensive line tear a post right out of the boardwalk from its foot-long bolts. On top of the post sat a basketball-sized golf ball with a slice cut out of it to keep scorecards. One guy walked away with it on his shoulder, Bamm-Bamm Rubble-style.

At the foot of an off-ramp, a police car pulled up the street.

• • •

Over the years, I've tried to figure out where things went wrong in high school, where I morphed from God-fearing, Phil Collins-loving honors student to Cadillac emblem-stealing, binge-drinking juvenile delinquent with spotty punk rock credibility. I used to think, much further into adulthood than I'd like to admit, that there were forces beyond my control, that it was acts of God and socioeconomic pressures that pushed me over the divide.

This, of course, is delusional crazy talk. There's a scene in *Repo Man* where Duke, a skinhead punker, lies dying, shot after robbing a liquor store. His friend, Otto Maddox, played by Emilio Estevez, cradles him in his arms. "I know a life of crime led me to this sorry fate," Duke tells Otto. "And yet I blame society. Society made me what I am."

"That's bullshit," Otto says. "You're a white suburban punk, just like me."

• • •

The truth was I still liked Phil Collins at the time I stole Cadillac emblems, and society didn't force me to drink beer bongs and stand lookout for jocks while they vandalized a miniature golf course. But for our dramatic purposes, we could do a lot worse than point to the moment a spotlight from an Ocean City rent-a-cop's car blinded my eyes as a key moment of transformation.

Everyone got away—except for me and a pair of slow-footed linemen. Both jocks were 18. They were arrested, processed, and released. I was 17, still a minor, and was held in the jail overnight until I could get a parent or guardian to pick me up.

When I called home, Mom took the details down, calmly, seriously. Then she started to cry. Dad grabbed the phone from her hand.

"Don't tell the cops anything," he said. I hardly recognized his voice. He sounded hyper. "You didn't do a goddamned thing."

• • •

Before I went into the cage, I handed over my wallet and keys at the desk. They made me take the shoelaces out of my sneakers. "That's so you don't try to hang yourself," a cop explained. Killing myself was exactly what I wanted to do, for fear of what Mom was going to do to me.

No one else was in the cell. I put a roll of toilet paper under my head and tried to sleep on a bench. The ceiling spun around. I prayed I wouldn't throw up. Some girls from the party walked by and peeked in the window from the street. The sun was just coming up. They didn't say hi, lest they looked like accomplices. They just gawked. Cherry Hill girls were like that.

• • •

Mom was still teary-eyed when she got to Ocean City. Grandpop drove. His silence was odd; I don't remember him saying anything. We didn't get in the car. Instead, we walked up Ninth Street to the Chatterbox Diner, open 24/7, and we ordered eggs and bacon all around.

＊　＊　＊

The two linemen were sentenced to 100 hours of community service, and later hit me up for money to kick in for a new golf ball post. I declined. I attended youth counseling sessions in some Burlington County rehab center, which seemed punishment enough. At the first meeting, Mom and Grandmom came with a folder filled with report cards to show that, other than the golf ball incident, I was a good kid.

Mom and Dad sat me down to tell me I had been grounded for the rest of the summer, except for working at the car wash. The following fall, my SAT score dropped 120 points from the PSAT test score taken the year before. I was no longer a genius, if I ever was.

Notes on Colestown Cemetery: Two Sestinas

These next Notes will be about drinking.

. . .

This is about me drinking with my friends from high school, 17 years old, dodging cars crossing Route 38 on ten-speeds and Huffys. This is about us hiding behind bushes across from a dive bar and sending in Jimmy, all muscles and cheesy mustache, with a handful of singles to get us beer so we could go drinking.

This is about us drinking after Jimmy came out the side door of The Mill Road Inn with a shit-eating grin, three cases stacked under his arms, and we all got back on our bikes, twelve-packs bungeed over handlebars, as we made our way back to the west side of Cherry Hill. We were Irish kids *heavily into puberty* with names like Pete and John and Shawn and Jimmy, sneaking sips of the first can with a straw.

. . .

This is about us drinking as we followed dark trails past the swim club, past the half-pipe built by kids from Cherry Hill West, and into Colestown Cemetery, the only green space we could find.

We set up camp beside our favorite headstones—names with birthdays we celebrated, toasted to, waved flags for.

This is still about us drinking Old Milwaukee, the cheapest beer available to mankind—and don't tell me about Milwaukee's Best or Keystone or Schaeffer, this is the fricking 80s we're talking about, it's Old Mildew all the way. It's the only beer that tastes skunkier as it gets colder.

This is about us drinking and having a contest to see who could crush a can against our forehead.

This is still about us drinking and also about how we skipped Sunday night mass, shotgunned cans with a screwdriver in St. Pete's parking lot, flagged down 12-year-old boys and asked what the priest's homily was about in case our moms quizzed us.

This is about us drinking Old Milwaukee in Cherry Hill, in Colestown Cemetery, on the corner of Church Road and Kings Highway, as Van Halen plays from a boombox.

This is about us bringing girls—actual, nonimaginary girls— to drink beside our favorite headstones.

This is about us skinny-dipping in the swim club next door, where we waved limp hot dogs over the fence to throw guard dogs off-scent. This is about us drinking Old Mildews in Colestown Cemetery, leaping off the high-dive at midnight, out of our fucking gourds, and somebody singing Van Halen.

This is still about us drinking Old Milwaukee in Colestown Cemetery in Cherry Hill, listening to Van Halen on the boombox, and one of us spotting headlights coming closer, six blocks away, five blocks away. And when we realized it was the cops, we finished our beers, ran like fucking hell, and ditched our bikes in the flower patches.

. . .

This is about the one time we were nabbed, and then questioned by the cops. We gave then fake names—how did we not get our heads clocked by them? We giggled in their faces as they wrote the names down.

My name, officer, is *Ben Dover*, my name, officer, is *Willy Feltersnatch*. My name, officer sir, is *Phil McCracken*.

. . .

This is about drinking then heading home on a bike that weaved along Cherry Hill's smooth streets, its weedless lawns, and straight-edged sidewalks. I wondered about the split-levels with bright kitchens, bumper pool tables, inground pools.

. . .

And this is about biking past Benash Liquors, down Coles Avenue, where I stopped to throw up in a bush, happy to be back in Maple Shade, where even the air seemed rough to the touch.

62.

Notes on *Purple Rain*

I accepted a double date invitation from Bruce Chace to go to Cherry Hill East's junior prom. There's no other way to put it: Bruce was swishy. He wore immaculately tailored suits and lived in a McMansion's guest house that had a hot tub. We weren't really friends, so I can't figure out why I escorted a blind date as a favor, along with Bruce Chace and his beard. My best guess is I'd just gotten my driver's permit and had a car, the Country Squire station wagon, which I rechristened the "Love Boat."

A biblical rain came down that night. I dropped off Bruce and our dates; I then drove the Love Boat into the rain, lost and drunk, and sang along to my *Purple Rain* cassette 30 miles into the Jersey Pines. I took the station wagon deep into Cherry Hill, past Evesham and Ramblewood, way beyond Tabernacle.

New Jersey is so small, I thought. If I just turned around, I'd eventually find home.

◆ ◆ ◆

Purple Rain's total running time is 43 minutes and 51 seconds, and those familiar with the film's soundtrack know the emotional *winterreise* Prince and the Revolution take the listener on: from "Let's Go Crazy," to the *do-you-want-him-or-do-you-want-me* of "The Beautiful Ones," to the caterwaul of "Darling Nikki" and falsetto finale of "Purple Rain." I sang along to it all, and in the process just got more and more lost.

Half crying, I cursed out loud, *fuck fuck fuck*, and pulled into a Wawa parking lot, the inky sky full of stars. Some Piney kid who worked there played Ms. Pac Man in the corner. He didn't know how to get back to the highway.

I called home collect. Dad picked up.

"I'm lost," I said. "I can't even find the name of the road I'm on."

He asked where I was, and so I looked outside and tried to read the signs. I couldn't. He asked me where I thought I was, and I told him the air smelled like cow shit.

He told me to look up at the sky. "Can you find the North Star?"

It felt like we were back in the backyard, looking though the telescope. I started to laugh.

"Find the Big Dipper," he said. "Look for the two stars at the end of the bowl. Follow the line over to the tip of the Little Dipper. And you'll see it: Polaris, the North Star."

"Then," he said, and this part I remember hearing through the rain, "go the other way."

Notes on the Empty Driveway

There was, finally, inevitably, the morning when Dad didn't come home. That morning was Thursday, October 31, 1985.

. . .

The day was sunny, pushing 70 degrees. When I got back from school, I walked inside, looked out past the spider plants in the bay window, onto an empty driveway. His car wasn't there, but that wasn't a surprise. Maybe he was back at the Sharon Motor Lodge. Dad had started hanging out with his friend—I have to repeat that, *hanging out with an actual friend*. Jimmy, a Maple Shade cop who worked nights, would close Jay's Elbow Room with Dad. Even Officer Jimmy didn't know Dad's whereabouts.

The question for the next three days: Where's Mike? Where's he gone?

. . .

There were signs, obvious and ignored. Our single piece of luggage, a yellow American Tourister, had gone missing. A couple years before, the Sisters of Saint Joseph chipped in and gave it to Mom so she could pack her clothes with some dignity.

. . .

We were just about to file a missing person report when Dad called on day four. He was at his sister Elena's house in Tucson, Arizona. It was 3 a.m.

His voice shook as he explained what he did. He packed the yellow suitcase, drove the primered van to Philadelphia International Airport, and bought a one-way ticket to Tucson.

"And I'm staying," Dad said.

Mom's back slid down the kitchen wall as she held the receiver. "This can't be happening! You can't be doing this!" she cried. "You have to come back."

"I'm not coming back," he said.

✦ ✦ ✦

Grandmom saw Dad the day before he left.

"His eyes were daggered and wide open," she told me. His usually neat, combed-over hair flew in the wind, and he "looked like a crazy man."

"He kept saying to me 'I'm trapped, I gotta get outta here. I gotta get outta here.' And I just said, 'Then go. Do what you gotta do.' "

Grandmom brought him out a can of beer. He downed it on the front porch, handed the empty to her, and left.

Notes on the Apple Trees

"You have to be able to forgive," Father O'Brien, our pastor, told Mom. "You can't bring the person you're trying to forgive down to their knees."

Mom could not forgive. My father could not be brought to his knees.

The year before he left, whenever things got especially bad, Dad had gone back to the Sharon Motor Lodge. This was also where he met Leanne for their continued rendezvous. The previous July, while our family shacked up down the Jersey shore in a small house in Avalon, Mom went back home and broke into my father's briefcase. In it, she found pictures of Leanne's baby.

"This was an ongoing relationship," Mom said. "This was not like getting drunk in the bar with some slut. He felt responsible for that kid."

• • •

In the weeks after his exit, people visited us, as if to pay their respects. Henry Styble, one of Dad's coworkers, sat at our table for two nights. He told Mom that all the guys in the truck barn knew what he was doing.

"The dock was a party at night," Henry said. "Beer and pot. We would get high and have a ball."

The second night, Harry brought his own beer—Bud tallboys. He got more emotional. The conversation turned ever so slightly.

"This is wrong," Henry kept saying. "Just so wrong."

"You're a good woman," he said to Mom, almost in tears. "You're too beautiful of a woman for him to do this to you."

Was Harry hitting on my mother? This marked the first time I felt the need to police my own house, to take control of an adult situation. Henry Styble had worn out his welcome. I walked toward him, smelled his sweet beer breath, and helped him get into his car.

* * *

"She wasn't a bad-looking girl," Mom told me. "I saw her once."

Another revelation, 20 years on. I press Record.

"I had to go in there and get his last paycheck. Grandmom went with me. I saw her from behind. She was wearing a black lace top, her bra straps exposed. The Madonna look."

"Did you confront her, approach her?" I asked.

"No," she said. "She did leer back at me, though. I was nothing like I am now. I was quiet, sedate, shy, easily intimidated. Menopause does wonders. It's freeing. I wasn't a crude, fighting-type person like I am now.

"I would never blame the woman. It was the man's choice. He made a bad decision. And it messed him up for the rest of his life."

* * *

"Nobody in our family trusts men anymore. Me, my sisters, your sister. Not after Mike left."

* * *

I think about that empty driveway every Halloween: the overgrown grass, oil stains. Meri calls it our "Abandon-iversary."

Behind our house, two crabapple trees, descendants of Maple Shade's orchards, filled with fruit each fall. Through my window, I would hear three or four apples at a time thump to the ground.

I spent nights out in the backyard, chucking those apples at the Little League's left field fence. A full 20 feet high, it looked more like a monster as the nights grew dark. I threw to hear the apples squish into chain links. I threw until my shoulder got so sore I couldn't use a pen at school. The biggest ones hung there through winter. The fence got so apple-filled it blocked out the moon.

Notes on the Primered Van

Over those three days while Dad was missing, Meri and I went about our business. We drank too much beer in the woods behind the furniture store across the street from the mall. At a keg party in the Jersey Pines, I jumped off a tire swing and broke a toe.

. . .

We had known, on some level, Dad would leave. Call it juvenile intuition.

The truth is, once he left, we were relieved. He was gone. And not just gone—he was across-the-country gone.

. . .

The morning after his phone call, Uncle Mark and Uncle Frank went to pick up the primer-covered van at the airport. The van ran out of gas when they crossed over to Jersey.

"Fucking Mike," Uncle Frank said when he brought the van back. "Couldn't even leave enough in the tank to make it home."

Inside was Dad's notoriously expensive $80 pair of work boots. Mom gave them to Frank for his trouble. They weren't my size anyway.

⋅ ⋅ ⋅

Dad had placed a note on the van's dashboard. I didn't know
about this note for 20 years, until one day it popped out of one of
Mom's files. It read, in large letters,

PLEASE DON'T TAKE

THIS VAN AWAY—

MY SON WILL

BE HERE TO

PICK IT UP

For months, I looked at the yellowed note, trying to crack its
code, to explicate it like some modernist poem: three syllables
each line except for the second line's four; the Emily Dickinson-
like long dash in line two; the random capitalized words, one
each line, like from a German translation; the forced dactyl, the
forced trochee, everything forced. It is, in short, a really shitty
found poem.

"Why didn't I pick up the van?" I asked.

"You had school to go to," Mom said. "I wasn't about to let you
play hooky just to get a crappy child-molester van in the airport
parking lot."

⋅ ⋅ ⋅

Dad had assumed that, since I would take over as Man of the
House, I would retrieve his abandoned vehicle, like when Pa on
The Ranch left his horses behind and the oldest son took care of
them.

"Your father gave the lot attendant ten bucks," my mother
said, using air quotes now, quoting what he said on the phone,
"so 'no one would fuck with it.' "

I think: I wish he used *fuck* in the note, maybe capitalized it. It would have made for a better poem.

· · ·

Thinking about this note this way reminds me of how Shader Record Nerds obsessed over the album cover of the Who's *Who Are You*. The band posed for its 1978 album in front of a scrap heap of old electrical equipment. Keith Moon, the band's brilliant and self-destructive drummer, sat on a chair, turned backward to cover up his gut from booze and drugs. Stenciled on the backrest in white spray paint are the words

NOT TO BE
TAKEN AWAY

Keith Moon died a month after the photo was taken. I remember how we saw this as some prophecy that Moon was going to leave the world.

Notes from Mom's Folder

There are some questions you ask and hope someone else can answer. There are other questions you know that no one can answer.

. . .

May 2010. My mother handed me a manila folder with a sticky note that said "For Danny," written in her immaculate cursive.

"Maybe these will help with, you know, your *memoir*." She pronounced "memoir" like "mem-wah," in exaggerated French, accompanied by a hand motion and a cigarette waved in the air. I must have jerkily corrected her pronunciation at one point.

. . .

Out from the folder comes a cascade of Polaroids from my senior trip to Disney World in Florida. Also inside were report cards from OLPH and Camden Catholic and follow-up letters from Burlington Country Juvenile Court after the golf ball arrest.

It occurred to me that she's handing over the last relics of my childhood.

. . .

The biggest item is a 1985–86 academic calendar. I flipped through. August and September 1985 are empty. Then the entries begin.

October 31, 1985: "Mike left us."

[Blank for November and December 1985].

January 10, 1986: "Flu."

January 11, 1986: "Flu."

January 12, 1986: "Flu."

January 13, 1986: "Flu. Dad [my grandpop] bought us tires."

January 14, 1986: "Ck. for heat assistance."

January 15, 1986: "Chrissy pregnant!"

January 16, 1986: "Look into getting own checking account."

January 17, 1986: "Job interview, Treitsman and Robin, 11:15 a.m., Phila."

January 20, 1986: "Treitsman and Robin, 4 p.m. 2nd interview."

January 21, 1986: "Got the job. Gave OLPH 2 wks notice."

January 27, 1986: "Meri sick"

The calendar chronicles my mother getting back on her feet, keeping her shit together, and finding a better-paying job. I ask Mom why she kept it.

"I just don't remember anything from that time," she said. "It was all such a blur. Maybe that's why I kept it: I wanted to remember what was going on. I didn't know one day to the next, one week to the next."

• • •

It's not on the calendar, but I stayed home sick on January 28, 1986. I'd faked it. Nobody cared if I went to school or not. I played records and ate peanut butter crackers. I turned on the TV. Live from Kennedy Space Center, the space shuttle Challenger sat on a launchpad. *Ten, nine, eight, seven, six, we have main engines start, five, four, three, two, one, and liftoff.* After a minute, the Challenger pivots and bursts into flames. The boosters trail off like bottle rockets. What was once intact had disintegrated. Chalk-white smoke pillowed through the Florida sky. The newscasters scramble to explain what had happened.

I felt nothing, as if I wasn't part of the same story that was on the screen. How was I able to detach myself from the world this way?

Some questions are fine left as questions.

67.

Notes on Father Destiny

The mailbox again overflowed with bills. Even with Mom's new job, we couldn't afford to keep the house. Mom warned me not to get hurt when I played basketball—we didn't have health insurance. We borrowed money for groceries, high school tuition, Meri's retainer. The collection agency calls started up again.

One lady from Sears called every day. "She kept saying 'I know you have money to pay this,' " Mom said. Her taunts drove her to tears. Years later, she still sounded angry over it. "I will never set foot in a Sears again. Never."

. . .

In the halls of Camden Catholic, people talked about college. Dorms. Overnights. My new girlfriend, Sherrie, whom I wooed while she played the lead in *Mame*, couldn't stop talking about her new roommate in Delaware. She planned on pledging a sorority. I tried not to think about college and in so doing thought about college all the time. The long-shot scholarships I went up for—La Salle, Villanova—didn't pan out. While it was nice to get admitted to the colleges I applied to—Penn State, Temple, Saint Joe's—I had no way to pay for it.

. . .

The college talk with Mom and Dad went something like this:
MOM
You're a smart kid. Very bright.

                    DAD
        You should go to college.

             END SCENE

                    •   •   •

Shortly after Dad left, I was called in for an appointment with
Camden Catholic's guidance counselor, a priest with a gray flat-
top and dark-rimmed glasses I nicknamed "Father Destiny."

                    •   •   •

My vision of college, if we could call it that, remained very
specific, in some ways modest, in others unrooted in any reality
except for the opening scene from *Revenge of the Nerds*. I'd drive
to Piscataway in a purple MG Midget convertible, milk crates of
records and clothes strapped inside an overflowing leather trunk.
I would then park on the same field where R.E.M. played. I'd wear
an overcoat and aviator goggle sunglasses, then hang out among
my fellow Rutgers New Brunswick students. I would strike up
lifelong friendships with other artsy kids from around the world.
    Father Destiny did not share this vision.

                    •   •   •

I walked into Father Destiny's office. He already had a folder
with my name stenciled on it. What did he have in my file? I pictured one of those cliché scenes from action movies, the clunky
exposition device where a villain's gendarme opens up the hero's
classified dossier—passport photo, transcripts, special-ops training photos, DISHONORABLY DISCHARGED stamped on top.
    "You don't seem to want to accept the fact you're dealing with
an expert in guerrilla warfare, a man who's the best with guns,
with knives, with his bare hands." That's how Richard Crenna's

character, Colonel Sam Trautmen, puts it to his superiors about renegade John Rambo. "A man who's been trained to ignore pain, to ignore weather, to live off the land, to eat things that would make a billy goat puke."

• • •

Father Destiny asked if my father had, in fact, left us, if we had trouble paying for Camden Catholic tuition. Yes to all, I replied.

"We need to change our game plan," he said. "Can't go away to college. That's a given. Too expensive."

Destiny got up and walked into another room. I took stock of my outfit: plaid pants,[12] bowling shoes,[13] velvet jacket,[14] piano tie,[15] and tuxedo shirt.[16] I was up for Class Comedian for the senior yearbook. It showed.

• • •

Our consultation was brief. Even with a full-blown case of Senioritis, my class rank held fast in the top 10 percent. As my beer-drinking buddies planned to attend Villanova, Penn State, and Fordham, Father Destiny advised me to attend Camden County College.

---

12 The Specials.

13 Paul Weller of The Jam.

14 Elvis Costello.

15 Joe Jackson.

16 The Cure.

. . .

CCC. C^3. Camden Catholic Continued. Kids at Paul VI High School called it Paul VII.

. . .

I decided to go full-time at the car wash instead.

. . .

Shaders didn't talk about college. They talked about which car they'd buy once they started working. A sociology book once classified Maple Shade as an epicenter of "Blue Chip Blues," "middle class people with working class values." Shaders are not strivers.

"As long as the kids can learn a trade and make some money at it, then we're happy," a Shader parent says. I didn't want to learn a trade and I didn't care about money. I just wanted out.

. . .

I dramatized the world in terms of John Hughes characters. In Cherry Hill's *Pretty in Pink*, I was a Ducky surrounded by Blanes. In Maple Shade's production, I was a Blane surrounded by Duckys. Really tough Duckys.[17]

---

17 Excerpted from agent's email, who passed on earlier manuscript of this book:

> I'm afraid we can't sell working class memoirs, much less by a white male with no drug addiction or criminal past...We do much better with upper-middle-class memoirs, such as ones by [Name Redacted] and [Name Redacted], preferably with a voyage of some sort, and a life lesson.

Best Regards,
[Agent Name Redacted]

PS You mention Moorestown, NJ. Wondering if you know [Name Redacted], an old college friend?

For one of my last term papers, I wrote about Plato's *Republic*. "Every kind of job will be picked according to their ability, or inability, to do certain things," I wrote on an index card. "At the lowest rungs will be workers, merchants, businessmen, clerks and farmers. Those who pass this first cut-off get ten more years of education and training. This will result in a second test, far more severe than the first. Those who fail will become the aides and lower rung soldiers."

In the margin, I wrote, "car washers?" I never had the chance to take Plato's second test.

68.

Notes on Autobiography:
An Aside

Once my father left, my life ceased to be interesting. In the months that led up to that week in October 1985, as Mike Nester packed, planned, and contemplated hauling his ass out of Jersey, my life teetered between breakdown and blossom.

Willa Cather once wrote, "Most of the basic material a writer works with is acquired before the age of fifteen." Graham Greene gives writers five more years. "For writers it is always said that the first 20 years of life contain the whole experience—the rest is observation."

For me that figure is 17 years, 7 months, and 28 days.

◆ ◆ ◆

Once the one myth of my father as a great man to emulate went away, all the others vanished with it—religion, love, loyalty to a place. I replaced them with records, books of my own, thoughts of my own. I'm still not sure if I've recovered. I'm not sure I want to recover.

Notes on Sergeant James

Sergeant James, the local recruiter based in Cherry Hill for the U.S. Army, must have gotten my number from Boys State, or when I registered for the draft, or from some career fair.

．．．

Sergeant James knew what my grades were. He knew my parents had split up. Did Father Destiny talk to Sergeant James? Sergeant James worked the long game, which was to get me to enlist in the Army when I turned 18.

．．．

Sergeant James knew I wanted to go to college—he knew where I applied, where I was accepted, and also that I couldn't afford it. He didn't call my friends. Sergeant James called me.

Sergeant James said I could go to college after I served out my enlistment. Or I could enlist in ROTC. Sergeant James's voice was smooth, like J.J. Jackson's. He called me "Sir" and "Mister Nester."

．．．

Sergeant James knew which buttons to push. An eight-year commitment? No way, I told him. "You don't want to work at the car wash for the rest of your life, do you, sir?"

. . .

Sergeant James visited me at the car wash once, an excuse to *drop off some literature*. He was dressed in civilian clothes: khakis, a tucked-in polo shirt. I put his red Mustang through the wash for free, with wax.

Sergeant James drove off the track, opened his window, and handed me a folder embossed with the U.S. Army logo, gave me a firm handshake.

That's the last time I saw Sergeant James. He must have given up.

70.

Notes on the Pennsauken Ping-Pong Story

Scot said we needed to go to Arlene's family's house in Pennsauken.

"So go," I said.

"You need to come along," he said.

We were shooting hoops. Scot parked his car behind the backboard, rolled down the windows, and played British New Wave.

"She needs to get clothes from her parents' place. I feel uncomfortable going with her alone."

Arlene and Scot had been dating six months, an eternity. How could he be uncomfortable?

· · ·

I had about five inches on Scot—point guard to my forward—so in theory, I should have been able to snuff Scot's shots and beat him 11-to-nothing. But Scot beat me every time. Scot asked personal or philosophical questions as we played. Just as he was about to take a jump shot, he'd ask me some deep question, some epistemological inquiry, and just as I would think up an answer, he would loft a shot over my head. *Swish.*

"I'm not sure I really want to go to college, not yet at least," Scot said, idly dribbling around the perimeter. "I'm not sure the American education system is for me. What do you think?"

I stop in my tracks. Maybe I *don't* need to go to college.

Scot took the shot. *Swish.*

It's difficult to describe Pennsauken to those who have never experienced Pennsauken. A stand-up comedian once said *Pennsauken* was the Native American word for "industrial park." Pennsauken is several towns in one: a goulash of upper-crust Cherry Hill and lower-crust Camden, and the glorious Pennsauken Mart, where you could buy military supplies, pose for a gang portrait, and eat the finest soft pretzels known to mankind, all under the same roof.

Arlene lived with her sister in an apartment complex in Pennsauken. The arrangement was strange. Why didn't she just live with her parents?

We pulled up to a split-level house. Arlene let us in. No one else was home. She went upstairs with empty bags to collect her clothes, and we sat down in the living room. The walls were filled with crucifixes and Mother Mary paintings; each piece of furniture was protected with clear plastic covers. I sat on a squeaky couch and Scot sat on a squeaky chair.

Scot stood up. "Let me show you something."

We walked down to the basement. It was finished with wood paneling from ceiling to floor and a tan rug that smelled like Lysol. He pointed to a couple holes in the wall.

"See these?" he whispered. "They're bullet holes."

He went back up the stairs to make sure Arlene couldn't hear us.

Six months ago, Arlene's parents were about to get a divorce. Her mom wanted it but not her dad. One night her dad came home, all crazy, shouting. They argued. They argued some more. He tied up Arlene and her sister in the kitchen and dragged her mom into the basement.

He shot her in the chest and killed her. After it sunk in what he'd done, and he heard his daughters screaming, he tried to shoot himself in the head, but missed. Then he ate handfuls of rat poison and tried to saw off his leg. Arlene and her sister untied themselves and ran out of the house. By the time the cops came, both parents were dead. Blood covered the basement floor.

◆ ◆ ◆

As Scot told this story, my mind went into a fog. We stood there not talking for a while.

"Hey, check this shit out," Scot said. He pointed to the center of the room: it was a ping-pong table. "This is a professional-grade net."

Scot slid his hands over the table, then handed me a racquet. "Let's volley for serve."

◆ ◆ ◆

"I really care about Arlene," Scot said, taking a backhand shot. "But do you think it should matter that our interests are compatible? I mean, she has Taylor Dayne cassettes, for Christ's sake."

I realized Scot was doing the asking-important-questions-while-playing-sports tactic. He returned with a wicked topspin. I missed.

"Yes!"

Arlene called down for us, and we sat back down on the squeaky furniture, a little ashamed.

◆ ◆ ◆

In my journal for this day, I wrote COPING MECHANISM?

My number one fear was that I would hit a ping-pong ball through a bullet hole, and it would cross over to the other side. We would then have to stop playing and deal with our idle minds.

71.

Notes on Being Voted Class Comedian

In the yearbook photo of Camden Catholic High School's 1986 Class Comedians, I wear a pair of tropical-printed shorts. I have a tie around my head. For the occasion, I'd brought along my first guitar, a knockoff fireglo Rickenbacker bought for 25 bucks. I pose with my left hand on the guitar neck and point at the camera with my right, a lame reenactment of Eddie Van Halen's pose on the back of *Women and Children First*. My female counterpart, a jester from the Pennsauken big hair contingent, stands to my left. In this context, she resembles Michael Anthony in drag. She wears a tie around her neck, and crosses her arms in a B-boy stance.

◆ ◆ ◆

The honor was not unexpected. I've always wanted attention, always milked jokes. The way I socialized in high school, the way I communicated my nervous energy, was through jokes, doing stupid shit, pulling hyperactive pranks.

◆ ◆ ◆

My comedy canon from this time: Steve Martin, Robin Williams, Richard Pryor, George Carlin, Cheech and Chong, Albert Brooks, Woody Allen, Eddie Murphy, Martin Mull, Sam Kinison, Whoopi Goldberg, Monty Python, National Lampoon's *Lemmings*, Steven Wright, Bob Newhart, Gilda Radner, *This Is*

Spinal Tap, Jonathan Winters, David Letterman's daytime show, Mel Brooks, Don Rickles, Lenny Bruce, Dick Gregory, Rodney Dangerfield, Lord Buckley, and "Weird Al" Yankovic.

• • •

Comedies don't need plots; leave that to thrillers and mystery. In *Mimesis*, Eric Auerbach writes about the "separation of styles," how it's comedy that was given exclusive rights to depicting everyday life: farts, boogers, sex. Life doesn't have a plot; like history, it's just one damn thing after another.

• • •

My classmates voted me Class Clown as well, but another senior, Ron Granucci, put the kibosh on a double-title win. Ron Granucci was the kind of guy who took a dump outside the back door of school and thought it was funny. His twin sister edited the yearbook. She eliminated the title entirely.

• • •

My take on comedy was the hokey, brown-noser variety. Bits and set pieces ranged from emphatically raising my hand, Arnold Horshack-style, to ribald comments in a Morris Day voice and air guitar routines in the hallways.

In class, I took up untenable, contrarian positions, sabotaged moot court with double entendres. Mr. Cabico singled me out to read my Language Arts vocabulary quiz sentences aloud. I used this opportunity to work in names like "Seymour Hiney" and "Dick Hertz." I was regarded as relatively harmless, albeit annoying and embarrassing.

• ◆ •

There were moments of what counselors would call "acting out" or "projective identification." Ms. Pizzalo, our chemistry teacher, whose desk bore a wooden plaque that read LACK OF PREPARATION ON YOUR PART DOES NOT CONSTITUTE AN EMERGENCY ON MY PART, genuinely hated me, especially when I used Bunsen burners as a blowtorch and made disingenuous faces. I sent Valentine carnations to football players and signed them with rivals' girlfriends' names. In health class, I giggled through a teacher's Vatican-compliant lecture on the benefits of the rhythm method and "taking vaginal temperature." I outgrew Catholicism one joke at a time.

• ◆ •

I never really got into trouble until spring. Someone pulled my toga down at an Animal House-themed pep rally. My butt flashed all the freshmen. As I waited outside the vice principal's office, Ms. Pizzalo walked by.

"You've had it coming for a long time," she said, very happy with herself.

I couldn't help but agree. By then I'd gotten every title I would ever earn.

ACT

THREE

72.

Notes on Grief:
Third Acts

Third acts suck. They introduce unlikely twists; they force you to wrap things up too tidily. They kill comedies. Comedies are about types; masks people wear (Bugs Bunny in a dress, Scooby Doo behind the tree) don't help with resolutions.

For years, I've been reading about plots, plot structure, and plot devices, hoping some of it would take. These Notes add up to a comedy, I hope.

• • •

My father died in his sleep. A last, massive stroke. Items on the desk in his apartment on the day he died:

A bottle of Evan Williams whiskey, one-third full

A leather-bound "Self Pronouncing" pocket Webster's Dictionary with our childhood signatures in it

Two Bic lighters (one pink and one black)

Plastic statues of Jesus and Saint Augustine

One pair of black-framed reading glasses

A bottle of Old Spice cologne

A pack of Lucky Strikes

There would be no burial. Dad specifically requested not to be embalmed or have a service. The one insurance policy he did sign up for took care of his cremation. It was with a company called Neptune, "America's Most Trusted Cremation Services." I thought it was one of the crazy schemes he'd bought into when I was growing up, but Neptune was legit. His body was transferred to South Lawn Cemetery in Tucson, the same place where Dr. and Mrs. Murlin Nester were buried. His only wish was to have a bench placed near their graves. He had even met with my aunt to show what kind of bench he wanted: concrete, with a naval insignia and his name. He left no money to pay for it, however, and my sister didn't have the cash.

His ashes were transferred to a naval ship in San Diego, the U.S.S. *Comstock*, and scattered two weeks later. Neptune asked us what words we would like said when his ashes were scattered, perhaps a prayer. Meri suggested a phrase he repeated often when we were kids, which totally dumbfounded us. He had it ironed onto a t-shirt at the Ocean City boardwalk: *Klaatu barada nicto*. It's the "I come in peace" greeting uttered by the alien in *The Day the Earth Stood Still*.

73.

Notes on The Jade

Growing up, Mary's Café was called the Jade Tavern, a dive bar on the outskirts of town. On the fifth celebration of Martin Luther King, Jr. Day in 1988, a *Philadelphia Inquirer* reporter came back to The Jade, as it was called, to see if anyone remembered Ernest Nichols and his encounter with King. The Jade "is the kind of pub that doesn't forget a birthday," the story begins.

"Yep," one patron, described as an "old prizefighter," said, drinking a Bud. "Ol' Ernie Nichols got his gun."

"You sure who got the gun, King or Ernie?" asked another man at the bar.

"No, ol' Ernie got the gun and chased him outta here," said another, who wouldn't give his name.

◆ ◆ ◆

By my senior year, Scot was out of high school, working for a wine importer and putting in days at his parents' liquor store in Pennsauken. Back in the 1950s, Mr. Harter used to make deliveries to Mary's Café. The proprietor barked orders as he signed for kegs of beer and soda water.

"That Ernie Nichols, he was one tough old German." Mr. Harter says. "No one messed with him."

◆ ◆ ◆

The last incarnation of Mary's Café was the Moorestown Pub, a name that's hilarious to anyone from Maple Shade. In a town with bars with names like The Jug Handle and Jay's Elbow Room, any place with the word "Pub" sounds pretentious. And then there's the Moorestown part. Maple Shade's neighbor is still one of the country's wealthiest towns, named by *Money* magazine as the nation's Best Place to Live. It is also a dry town founded by Quakers.

•   •   •

The Moorestown Pub closed and was then bulldozed to make a ramp onto Route 73. In the book titled *Maple Shade*, the town's entry in the popular Images of America series, a 2003 photo taken by local historian Dennis Weaver mentions its former name as Mary's Café, and that it was "set to be razed for a road project in 2008." There is no mention of Martin Luther King, Jr.

While the bar was set to be bulldozed, a local historian started a petition to place a plaque memorializing the King incident. Even if he was successful, there would have been trouble finding a curb or swatch of grass to stick anything in the ground. Real history gets paved over in places like Maple Shade.

•   •   •

I turned up one night at another bar, the Alden Café, to have a beer before meeting up with friends. It was early, and I met some guys who were ahead of me in school. They remembered my sister. I drank a Coors Light and watched the Flyers game. We started talking about CYO and Little League. Somebody recognized me from the car wash. The King story came up. An old-timer chimed in. King and his friend should've known better, he said.

"You don't go to The Shade," he said, "much less a local bar at one o'clock in the morning, if you're a black guy."

It remains unclear to me if this man was talking about 1950 or the present day.

74.

Notes on Rutgers-Camden

In 1949, Arthur Armitage, president of The College of South Jersey, offered to rename his college. His price? A million dollars.

"We are not so enamored with the name," Armitage told the *New York Times*, "that we wouldn't be very glad to change it if some wealthy person wants to make a generous endowment."

Armitage got his million dollars the next year when his college was absorbed into Rutgers University.

Thirty-six years later, in late August, I stood in line in the basement of Armitage Hall to register for classes.

♦   ♦   ♦

Nothing prepared me for Rutgers-Camden's blighted neighborhoods—not Camden Catholic, not Maple Shade, not the car wash. If there was one disclaimer the admissions office owed its prospective students, it was that Rutgers-Camden wasn't a college at all. It wasn't even a satellite campus. It was more like a compound of concrete at the base of the Ben Franklin Bridge, an outpost with a Rutgers sign. This was Rutgers for suburbanites like me who wouldn't trek up the Turnpike to the real Rutgers in New Brunswick, a mid-sized city with 40,000 students and Division I sports teams.

In a city that's more than 70 percent black and Latino and 40 percent below the poverty line, Rutgers-Camden was 75 percent white, the whitest and richest of all Rutgers campuses. Save two frat houses, no one dared sleep in Camden. Shiny cars from the suburbs hightailed down Cooper Street after class.

With me in the line were other ne'er-do-wells who put off registering until the last minute, kids who had partied too much at Brown or Temple, and people late for mall jobs they worked at so they could pay for their car so they could drive to their jobs at the mall.

* * *

An advisor signed me up as a Management-Marketing major. I was accidentally registered for an upper-level class called "Organizational Behavior." Held at night in a lecture hall filled with adults in business suits, I stood out like some jester dressed in plaid pants and a shirt from a local deli that read "On a Roll, You Can't Beat Our Meat." Beneath that slogan, an R. Crumb-like character masturbates a hoagie between his legs. I had started smoking pot at the car wash, which didn't help me focus for our group projects.

* * *

At the start of my freshman year, Rutgers embarked on an experiment: its first student dorm building. The Rutgers-Camden Apartments, an orange-brick box with room for 520 students, opened in September 1986. Behind 12-foot fences, the dorms resembled the county prison a couple blocks away. The dorms filled up with freshmen from North Jersey and law students from South Jersey. I put myself on the waiting list, and moved in that spring.

Many dorm students left Rutgers-Camden after their first year, when they realized they lived in a place where even Domino's Pizza didn't deliver. But there were also the ones who stayed, Goths and stoners and artfags, painters who rented spooky old houses off-campus. They liked the empty Camden streets and pay phones that rang at all hours. These were the people who became my friends.

75.

Notes on Au Pairs

I met my first real girlfriend while she was hitchhiking. I was driving the primer-painted van around Cherry Hill when I beheld seven young women beside Route 70, all in short skirts, all with their thumbs up. What red-blooded, 19-year-old American male would not pull over in this situation?

Before I could even say hello, the girls piled in the van. A blonde sat in the passenger seat. I pegged her as their leader. She wore a sailor shirt straight out of *Breathless*.

"*Vee are go-eeng to zee coastline!*" she said. "*Can you take us zere?*"

"*Eet eeez a club,*" another girl in the back said. "*Ze Coastline. Eet is down ze road.*"

"Just drive!" another shouted, this time in clear English.

I drove the girls to the Coastline, a nightclub where disco never died and people had out-of-wedlock sex in the parking lot. The girls were au pairs, live-in nannies from Europe. As we pulled in the parking lot, I heard the bass-thump from the Coastline's dance floor. The au pairs invited me along, but I passed. I'm 19, I told them, and don't have a fake ID. I did ask the blonde sitting in the front seat for her phone number.

• • •

Mette came from Copenhagen and spoke very little English, which was perfect for me. We dated seven months. We didn't have sex for a really long time. I was afraid I'd get her pregnant.

I'd hang out with Scot and his friends and describe these elaborate erotic situations we'd get in, how I had Mette's clothes off in the van, or how she'd do things to me in a movie theater, or how I'd spend hours rubbing her breasts. Scot would sit there, quaking.

"But did you *fuck* her? Jesus, my dear boy, *lay some pipe!*"

· ◆ ·

Back in the 80s, au pairs arrived in South Jersey with a suitcase and an address to their family's house. They bought winter clothes once they got here. Au pairs spent their days changing diapers for Cherry Hill families. At night, au pairs got to boogie down at places like the Coastline and drink champagne bought for them by old men. They crafted ludicrously fake IDs out of Swedish library cards. Not that any self-respecting South Jersey bouncer would turn away a gaggle of chicks in short dresses with foreign accents.

Au pairs traveled in packs. Most didn't get to use their host families' cars. If one au pair lined up a ride somewhere, they felt obligated to bring the others. Dating Mette, then, meant I also dated Veronique, Lotte, Sigrid, and others. Scot and a couple other friends went out with a series of these girls thanks to this arrangement.

· ◆ ·

As quickly as it started, Mette and I came to an end. We had sex finally, and I'm sure I was twice as awful and unskilled a lover as I prefer to remember. Soon after, we had our first argument. Mette went off to the Coastline and she never called me back. I wasn't heartbroken as I was confused, and I'd be lying if I said my life as an au pair pimp didn't take the sting out of my life as a loser commuter student who washed cars.

76.

Notes on Quitting

I have in front of me a clipping from the *Burlington County Times*, dated 1986, titled, simply, "Car Wash." The photo feature describes the workers of Sunshine Wash 'n Buff as "the crew," eager workers who "will gladly make your wheels—and the rest of your car, too—look almost new with a little soap and water."

There's Bill, reattaching an antenna onto a Range Rover. There's Gary, wiping down the driver's side door of a Mercedes, about to give his send-off smile for tips. "Gary Smith finds that a little music helps him forget about the cold winds," the caption reads.

And there's 17-year-old me, looking super-serious as I stand against the wall. "Dan Nester tries to thaw his hands." My Limahl-like hair, fluffy with dark curls in back, looks yellow even in black and white.

◆ ◆ ◆

I never quite figured out what the deal was with Bill, the workaholic manager of Sunshine. Bill was my personal style icon: at school, I replicated his look of roach killer shoes, bright-colored Ray Ban knockoffs, and mesh-overlaid Chams du Baron shirts from the Chess King outlet. He wore Gazelle sunglasses, and had blond, curly hair like Willie Aames circa *Eight Is Enough*.

The story I heard about Bill was he got expelled for dealing pot in high school. I always suspected there was more. What motivates someone to work at a car wash 365 days a year for six years? Each winter morning, as salt-caked cars lined up along Camden Avenue, Bill rolled up the metal doors at sunrise, filled the buckets with soap concentrate, and pressure-washed frozen sludge along the track.

• ◆ •

I took off a couple weekends after high school graduation. When I got back, I figured out why Bill worked so hard: he bought the wash from Luigi. Everyone has a dream, and for Bill it wasn't to be a stoner who worked at a car wash; it was to be a stoner who worked at a car wash that he also owned.

• ◆ •

A few months later, there was a police bust. The story I was told was that Bill had gotten hooked on hard drugs—the track inside was filled with needles and used works. Luigi swooped back in and took over the wash. I never believed this account, and said so at the time. A couple months after Bill left, I worked for Ronnie, a Luigi flunky who took over as manager. People called him "Ronnie Tirebiter." I didn't know if he liked to bite tires, but I did know he was a major dick. He bossed me around a lot, probably because he regarded me as a Bill loyalist. Ronnie drove an Iroc Z Camaro, thought he was hot shit, and liked to talk about having sex with pregnant women.

"They have a glow," he'd say. "Plus, they can't get pregnant."

I'd browse his back issues of *Ready to Drop* magazine by the toilet and dry-heave.

• ◆ •

Ronnie implemented a new system in which I would scrub whitewall tires all day, just whitewalls, all down the line, slapping on soap from a five-gallon bucket and scrubbing each tire with a wire brush. Soaping and wire-brushing—all day. This freed up Ronnie to act like a manager and prance around with a clipboard and fool around with the track controls.

One Sunday, sick of wire-brushing whitewalls, I begged to switch jobs with anyone else.

"What about that guy?" I pointed to a wiper dude my age with a super-long mullet.

"He can't do it," Ronnie said. He scribbled on his clipboard. "Plus, he's new."

The new guy was a learning-impaired moron from another one of Luigi's washes. Brushing white walls, Ronnie explained, meant he couldn't smoke.

"Fine," I told Ronnie. "But my fucking arms are going to fall off."

He grabbed my shoulder. "First of all, don't curse at me." Then Ronnie picked up a ball-peen hammer off his desk. "Second of all, I'm gonna break your fuckin' kneecaps!"

I ran across Camden Avenue to the van, two middle fingers in the air. Giving notice didn't seem necessary. After the car wash, I never quit jobs. I just walked away.

77.

Notes on Arizona

I had a non-stellar freshman year. By spring semester, I was drinking beer and shots after morning classes at a Campbell Soup employee bar a couple blocks away from campus. I got a "D" in a biology class called "The Facts of Life." One night, at a new college catering job, I snuck into the master bedroom of a Rutgers-Camden trustee and called up Dad. He scolded me for mooching someone's long distance.

"Come out West and live with me for a couple weeks," he said. "Drive my truck out in the desert while I'm at work."

To entice me, he mailed black-and-white photos of his guns.

. . .

He bought me train tickets because they were cheaper than flying. When finals were over, Mom dropped me off at 30th Street Station. I spent four days in coach: four days staring at corn stalks and Texas flatlands, four days drinking myself to sleep. I had clumsy sex on the floor of a handicapped bathroom with an Illinois cheerleader.

The Arizona visit marked the first time I didn't have a job since fifth grade. I'd drop Dad off at the truck terminal and drove his International Scout out into the desert, U2's *The Joshua Tree* on cassette. We ate burritos the size of dachshunds.

• • •

In Arizona, your guard is up at the same time you feel the freest. Arizona is also a place where you can be alone in a very intense way, and that's why, I think, my father returned there.

Arizona is not Walden. Arizona is a moon colony. It's a place unsuitable for normal human existence. That's why it's the perfect place to be exiled.

• • •

Dad and I went into the desert to shoot guns. His .45 pistol kicked me to the ground. I fired an automatic with a big magazine, a Tec-9, into a hunk of plywood.

• • •

Toward the end of my stay, I spent three afternoons in a dentist's chair to take advantage of Dad's Teamster coverage. The hygienist, a woman with dirty-blonde hair and a raspy voice, stared into my eyes as she prepped me for each day's drilling and filling. We flirted. The office still used real laughing gas, and I remember how I'd sit back, loopy, listening to the piped-in music. She stroked my hair, looked into my eyes as she put the mask over my nose. Her breath hit my neck as she sang along to Willie Nelson's rendition of "Help Me Make It Through the Night."

She invited me to meet up for a drink, to get some "real margaritas." But I got cold feet. She seemed so old to me—she couldn't have been older than 30—and I felt the pairing with this California divorcée would be unnatural. When the nitrous oxide spell broke, instead of following directions to her house, I pointed the International Scout to the desert and blasted more U2 as part of some Bono purification process.

226

78.

Notes on Killer Lawnmowers

The last thing I wanted to do when I got back from Arizona was to sculpt the lawns of the South Jersey bourgeoisie. But I needed a job, the van was dead, and my prospects were limited. My boss, Mr. Jacks, lived in The Shade and went to our church. He shined his brights outside at 5:30 a.m., and I'd stagger out to a cup of coffee from his thermos. He played Howard Stern, which took up the space where I might've blabbed on about how I smoked pot or was thinking about becoming an English major.

◆ ◆ ◆

Professional landscapers work with walk-behind mowers. Two rear wheels drive the mowers forward. Each wheel is controlled by a clutch handle that puts the mower in and out of gear. To stop, the landscaper pulls both clutch handles and locks them into place. The locks are really just clasps, and sometimes they break free, which the operator must correct, so long as the mower doesn't get away first.

If this sounds like telegraphing, that I'm trying to tell you something bad is about to happen, you guessed correctly.

◆ ◆ ◆

One mid-August morning, I finished off a lawn's strip of grass between the sidewalk and the curb. I stopped the mower, locked the clutches' clasps. In an instant, the left-side clasp snapped loose and sent the wheel into gear. I tried to reach down to turn the blades off, but the mower had gotten away. It turned around in a tight circle.

One of the mower's blades nipped the heel of my right sneaker and cut my Achilles tendon. All it took was a slight brush of the blade's tail end. If the mower hadn't hit a curb first, it would have taken another swipe at me, that time over my chest, since by then I was on my back inspecting what I thought was a small cut.

An ambulance peeled rubber down the quiet Moorestown street. One EMT put a needle in my arm before I was lifted onto a gurney. Another fainted when he looked at my dangling foot.

. . .

Mom left work and met me at the hospital. She was in tears, said *my baby my baby* over and over. We were relieved to find out that I could keep my foot.

Dr. Krall, a podiatric surgeon with a Sam Elliott mustache, explained the surgery. "Your tendon is like a rubber band," he said. I went in and out of a morphine stupor as he talked about the hole he'd cut in the back of my calf to snag the tendon and bring it back down my leg. Dr. Krall stretched a real rubber band to demonstrate. After the tendon was repaired, there would be a bump on my heel and five-inch scar.

. . .

In *The Iliad*, Paris shoots a poisoned arrow, guided by Apollo, into Achilles's heel, the only vulnerable part of his elaborate suit of armor. Unlike Achilles, I had no celestial armor from Ulysses to protect me. I wore cutoff jeans and a pair of Allesse tennis sneakers. The doctors said wearing work boots would've made my injury worse. The blade, tangled into thick leather, would have hit more nerves.

. . .

Though I say, "a lawnmower ran me over," it would be more accurate to say, "I operated a self-propelled lawnmower that, through neglect of a lawn care equipment industry more concerned with production costs than personal safety, possessed a serious design flaw that led to my being maimed."

The "self" in "self-propelled" is inaccurate. It would be more accurate to say the mower often runs off by itself. Not like the scene in *The Lawnmower Man*, when the former imbecile, his intelligence now ginned up by virtual reality, mind-controls his mower around a yard. We're talking all by itself, a solo lawnmower on the run.

. . .

There's a part of me that suspects I was run over by the killer lawnmower because of something I had done. That's the Roman Catholic part of me talking.

. . .

For the next two and a half years, I wore a polio brace that made me look like I had a prosthetic robot foot grafted onto a black Doc Martens shoe. Two cogs prevented the ankle from bending past 90 degrees. The brace made metallic clunks as I limped along. The figure I struck was Dickensian.

. . .

You might surmise I've thought a lot about this. So did my lawyer, a badass Italian American with gelled-back hair and a ponytail, whose daughter worked with me at the Rutgers-Camden *Gleaner*. He took one look at me—the brace, limp, and scars—and handed me his business card.

"These mowers," he said, putting his hands together at the points of his fingers, "are death machines. They've gotta pay."

79.

Notes on Point Street

The German philosopher and critic Walter Benjamin used the phrase "profane illumination" to describe surrealism. It's also the best way to describe living in Camden.

By the late 1980s, Reagan's second term, the world seemed like it was fucked. Something hung in the air. The music sounded compressed and distorted: gated drum sounds, noodly guitar solos, vocals drenched in reverb.

Hobbling around in my polio brace, I wrote shitty record reviews and preachy editorials for the student paper. "Our decade of the eighties has proven to be a hybrid of times past," I wrote in the *Gleaner's* October 1, 1986 issue. "The concept of being original or away from the mainstream is shunned, replaced by a bland sameness."

• • •

From 1986–1991, if you walked down Point Street, between Penn and Linden, five blocks from campus, you would have heard the following music blasting out of a window:

2 Live Crew's *Move Somethin'*

Public Enemy's *It Takes a Nation of Millions to Hold Us Back*

The Geto Boys' "Gangsta of Love"

Hüsker Dü's *Candy Apple Grey*[18]

---

18 a.k.a. the Most Depressing Album Ever Made.

Side One of *Let Them Eat Jellybeans!*[19]

Pantera, Kiss without makeup, W.A.S.P., Overkill

A homemade looped recording from The Butthole Surfers's cover of Black Sabbath's "Sweet Leaf," in which a male voice shouts *Satan! Satan! Satan!*

• • •

I moved into a row home on Point Street with two ex-pats from the Rutgers dorms. Derek, a stoner from Haddonfield, played synth keyboards in a hair band called Broken Heartt (the two t's intentional, cf. Ratt and Rough Cutt). He sold pot out of his bedroom. Nadine, a Goth girl who once made out with Billy Zoom from X, was an oncologist's daughter from Moorestown. She spent weekends at her boyfriend's house. The rent was $450 a month, split three ways.

Rutgers-Camden wasn't Hampshire, but with my eyes squinted, I could pretend this was a *real college experience*. We watched students and professors drive back to the suburbs, and took pride that we were the ones who chose to stay in Camden. We could claim we were punk rock because we lived in a city of abject poverty and run-down buildings. We were keeping it real. Or surreal.

• • •

The January 20, 1992, issue of *Time* featured a story on Camden, "Who Could Live Here?" "The story of Camden is the story of boys who blind stray dogs after school, who come to Sunday Mass looking for cookies because they are hungry, who

---

19 Punk compilation from the Alternative Tentacles label, with an image of Ronald Reagan on the cover; includes Dead Kennedys' "Nazi Punks Fuck Off," Bad Brains' "Pay to Cum," and The Feederz's "Jesus Entering From the Rear," arguably the most sacrilegious song ever recorded.

arm themselves with guns, knives and—this winter's fad at $400 each—hand grenades," *Time*'s Kevin Fedarko writes.

The Point Street stoner punks were tourists, but Camden didn't make distinctions after sundown. Bodegas sold individual eggs and cigarettes. Everything closed up except for liquor stores, their attendants protected by thick plastic walls. At night, kids rode mopeds in V formation to deliver crack. Campus cops cruised by frat houses to make sure no one strayed past what the college called, rather straightforwardly, the Safe Zone.

♦ ♦ ♦

Everyone I knew in those years played a role. Some of us were Joe Strummers or Sal Paradises, others Siouxsie Siouxs or Nancy Spungeons. We all tried out new personas from year to year. Metalheads taped posters of their favorite bands on their bedroom walls (Judas Priest, Iron Maiden). Burnouts played in a band called Vic Morrow and The Choppers and did acid all day. I was trying to be Allen Ginsberg, or some mash-up of all the Beats, except straight and with a mullet.

A group of artists and musicians lived in an old Victorian under the Ben Franklin Bridge. Most didn't go to Rutgers, but came to Camden to live on the cheap. Some were in a band called True Detectives that played live samples of music, reggae, rap, and metal. When they arrived, it felt like we had started our own scene or subculture. I hopped on the PATCO train to Philly with Nadine and Derek to see the True Detectives play clubs, and danced in little mosh pits in front of the stage. We called ourselves the Camden Crew.

. . .

During the day, the Crew walked past the bridge and explored the city. Words fail me when I talk about Camden's landscape, so I asked someone else to describe it. Josey, a guitarist who played in True Detectives, gave it a try. "Garbage was everywhere. Mountains of trash piled in the backyards of abandoned row homes, loose, unbagged. Even the *favelas* of Brazil were not so tragic, grim, and hopeless. No goofball installation artist could ever top it."

. . .

Derek put stems and seeds in a coffee grinder and sold it to frat brothers as bags of an exotic strain from Oregon. Our Division III Rutgers-Camden Pioneers basketball team, midway through its 117-game losing streak, the longest of any college team, bought pot on Point Street before and after games.

. . .

"My father's disappearance is going to creep up on me," I wrote to myself on November 27, 1988. "I feel a burning desire to get 'something' done."

How capable I was of complete self-absorption without any sense of irony! I was a 20-year-old English major and felt like I was running out of time. As T.S. Eliot might say, I was growing old and wore the bottoms of my jeans rolled.

Notes on
"Truck Driver Divorce"

"Truck Driver Divorce," Frank Zappa's mock country tune from 1984, begins with the lines: "Truck driver divorce! It's very sad! Steel guitars usually weep all over it." When I first heard it, I of course thought of my own family's hackneyed soap opera. But it wasn't until 1989 or so that the situation reached Zappa-scale absurdity.

Dad called every week to pressure Mom to sell the house. He'd gotten a union job with an affiliate of his company in Jersey. Getting a union job in Arizona was like finding a needle in a Republican "right to work" state haystack. His good luck had impressed me before I found out he'd planned his move for months.

. . .

The house sold for $75,900. The profits were split 50/40/10—mother, father, and kids. Mom paid off debts to grocery stores, doctors, schools, and credit cards. Meri and I bought used cars with our cuts of $1,250. The terms of the Nesters' divorce stipulated that Dad was also required to send child support—$100 a month—to Meri and me until we got out of college. He refused to send any money to either of us. Arizona was a nonreciprocal state for child support, and Mom's lawyer didn't have a clue what to do. "Divorce wasn't really his main thing," she said. Over the years, we thought about taking measures to garnish his wages.

Let it lie, one of us always would say eventually.

81.

Notes on the Ben Franklin Bridge

My LSD debut was an overplanned group affair. Twenty of us on the east side of Point Street planned to drop at the same time. We lined up several trip-friendly activities: places to visit, people to visit, music to play, things to freak out over. It began in Derek's room, where we listened to a carefully curated mix of mellow songs. We cut up a blotter that had rows of Bart Simpson holding a slingshot straight ahead.

• • •

Derek held up a CD of Dire Straits' *Brothers in Arms*. "This disc is DDD," he explained, worshipfully. "Digitally recorded, digitally mixed, and digitally pressed. It's never touched a tape before hitting our ears."

He passed the jewel box around, pointing to the letters on the tray card. We then listened to "So Far Away" in silence, which was borderline torture. But rules were rules: everyone got to pick a song, which the rest of us would have to listen without saying anything.

"Do you feel it yet?" Beverly, a painting major with white-blonde hair and blue strands, whispered to me.

"I think the stereo just made streaks," I said.

Beverly twirled the braided ponytail that sprouted out of her forehead. "It's the volume knob. It does keep spinning, doesn't it?"

• • •

She took my hand as her selection, Gary Numan's "Remember I Was Vapour," started. The synthesizer went in and out of my head. The drum machine matched my heartbeat. We held each other's hands and drank iced water. *There's nothing here but us,* Gary Numan sang. All of us saw streaks by the end of that song.

• • •

We grabbed 40s out of the fridge. Derek led us outside.

"Where are we going?" I asked nobody in particular. Beverly kept holding my hand. There's always a den mother in LSD groups, and in my experience it's usually a Goth girl.

"Just follow me," Derek said. He led ten of us over to the Walt Whitman Center a block away. Next to an empty fountain were symbols engraved in the metal tiles.

"Take a look," Derek said. His grin widened.

I squatted down and swept some moss away. "OH SHIT!" I said. "THOSE ARE SWASTIKAS!" I traced them with my hand and looked up to him, like I was Charlton Heston discovering a half-buried Statue of Liberty at the end of *Planet of the Apes.* "Why the fuck are they here!"

• • •

We skateboarded in one of General Electric's abandoned parking lots along the waterfront. The Ben Franklin Bridge's blue light waved up and down the puddles. On our side of the Delaware, piles of industrial garbage rose up from the ground like pyramids. As trucks barreled over from Philadelphia, the suspension cables plucked notes like some giant harp.

Holly was a punk rock girl from Moorestown who wore sundresses and purple Doc Marten boots. Crazy and beautiful, Holly had a rock promoter boyfriend, Barry, whom we all believed killed someone. A couple weeks earlier, Holly and I had hooked up. I was on the rebound: a Rosemont College philosophy student had just dumped me. I didn't invite Holly to the LSD party. She got mad.

That night, Holly sat on my front step with Beverly and Nadine. I tried to scramble past them to get up to my room.

Holly cut me off. "Hey Dan," she said. "Aren't you going to talk to me? Who do you think I am, your little arty whore?"

"Uh, I dunno," I said. I pictured Barry on his motorcycle, like Randall "Tex" Cobb in *Raising Arizona*, riding up the street to take me to some fiery underworld. "I'm not sure if I am speaking English right now."

Holly looked at me and growled. My brain hummed. In one of the most ungentlemanly acts I had ever committed in my life up until that point, I ran up to my room and locked the door.

• • •

The last thing you need when you're tripping on acid is to be alone. I went back outside. A tugboat on the Delaware sounded its horn. I ducked.

Then I looked up.

There were LASERS SHOOTING ACROSS THE SKY.

I looked down. Then up.

There were LASERS SHOOTING ACROSS THE SKY.

Up again.

There were still FUCKING LASERS FUCKING SHOOTING ACROSS THE FUCKING SKY.

· · ·

It would be another twenty years before I found out that night was when the City of Philadelphia tested its Fourth of July laser show by shooting them across the Delaware into Camden. Holly now works as a gardener in Utah. Beverly runs an animal shelter. Everyone does adult things. Camden is still Camden. Little kids still light drums full of garbage on fire. While I lived there I never felt more paranoid and alive.

82.

Notes on the Tale of the Toothless Ogre

The second-floor balcony of True Detectives' Victorian house juts out to Third Street. If you wanted to make a dictator-style speech to the Ben Franklin Bridge, that would be your spot. From there you could also peek over to Armitage Hall, the dull gray office compound where I sat through most of my classes.

Rutgers professors lingered or barreled through syllabi filled with Chaucer-Milton-Shakespeare, Joyce-Yeats-Eliot, *Middlemarch-Madame Bovary-An American Tragedy*. As I stood on that balcony watching cars go by, I could forget about which circumspect paper topic I would propose, or which chunk of *Bleak House* was due to be plowed through. My English department's dull cohesiveness made Catholic school look like Bard. It seemed absurd, living where and how I was, to read literature of Dead White Guys with Toni Morrison tacked on for the last week.

• • •

It was only after I started working nights at the library when I found writers who spoke to me. In the little magazines and smaller books, I found literature that was relevant, confrontational, revolutionary. We're talking of course about the Beats: Allen Ginsberg and Gregory Corso and William S. Burroughs. We're also talking about another, ad hoc mix: Sylvia Plath, Arthur Rimbaud, the Italian Futurists, Anne Waldman, John Giorno,

Frank O'Hara, Sharon Olds, Norman Mailer, Kathy Acker, Charles Bukowski, Adrienne Rich, and Amiri Baraka.

• • •

That balcony also marked the spot where I had my first bad acid trip. In a matter of months, I'd graduated to all four quarters of the Bart Simpson tab. We used to joke about *seeing God* and *feeling like God*. I didn't have time for God. In the True Detectives' house, I could feel like an artist or at least an English major who wore long scarves.

• • •

The bad trip night began with a spaced-out jam session in the True Detectives' basement. I went out to the balcony for fresh air. I noticed Beverly and a man walking home. Both swayed like drunks. And there he was: the Toothless Ogre.

• • •

He was an old guy with purple David Lee Roth pants and a half-shirt with a band logo on it. He had a couple teeth missing. He looked like a fat Don Dokken. He got past me, made his way down to the basement, and stood next to the drum set. He'd heard our racket and wanted to investigate. Someone asked, "Who is that Toothless Ogre downstairs?"

Me and the Detectives laughed. The Ogre heard. He got pissed.

"Where's my ma woman?" he shouted up the stairs. Beverly had hid herself in the kitchen.

The Toothless Ogre, in his mind, thought he he had sauntered into some haunted Scooby Doo house, and he met him some real, live Satanists. He looked at all the gear, the guitars humming against the amps, the microphones.

"Well, lookie here!" he shouted. "I'm gonna do whatever I want down here. I've been in rock 'n roll for a long time. You guys think you're special? I've been onstage at the Trocadero. I am a serious motherfucker!"

Our situation immediately felt desperate. We were abductees. And though everyone knows it's unwise to admit to tripping to non-tripping people, it's also the first thing people do when they're tripping.

"Hey man," Mikey, the drummer, whispered. "Be cool—we're all trippin' out."

The Ogre raised an eyebrow. He then challenged us to *a real battle of the bands*, like we were in a live-action production of "The Devil Went Down to Georgia." Nothing made sense except that the Toothless Ogre wouldn't leave. Inside our acid-tripping minds, the Ogre transformed into golem, a leprechaun with a mullet, Pinhead from *Hellraiser*, all wrapped into one.

The standoff lasted 30 minutes but seemed like 30 hours. Nadine and her friend Rita sat crying in the corner. Randy the bassist slipped me a crowbar and walked into a storage closet.

"Get ready," he said. "I'm getting my crossbow."

I am going to jail for manslaughter, I thought, *all for killing a fat Don Dokken.*

"I pictured the newspaper clip," Nadine wrote to me. "'Young Girl from Well-to-do Moorestown Family Slain in Basement of Camden Drug Den.'"

◆　◆　◆

Then, for some reason, I started to laugh.

"Dude, are you nuts? There are, like, seven of us. And one of you. You're drunk. And we're tripping our faces off. We don't care if we live or die right now. Get the hell out of here."

The Toothless Ogre paused for five seconds. Then he walked out. Everyone looked at me. I was the hero of the moment. I couldn't resist saying one more thing as he walked upstairs.

"It's only rock 'n roll, man."

Ogre returned to get his shirt back, which had a wad of money in it. Beverly threw it down from the balcony.

He found his money, which freaked him out more.

"We don't want your money!" Beverly shouted. "Just leave us!"

Ogre buttoned up his shirt. He then ripped it apart in some pseudo-voodoo gesture. Beverly took out a bible and read a random quote. The Ogre took off, spooked.

You can't out-Goth a Goth girl who keeps a live snake in her hair.

• • •

As the Ogre walked away, a pack of twenty wild dogs trotted down Third Street. They stopped, looked at us, and then kept going.

83.

Notes on Moby-Cock;
or The Term Paper

In the spring of 1989, I registered for a class called Melville and Pynchon. We were assigned two novels: Herman Melville's *Moby-Dick* and Thomas Pynchon's *Gravity's Rainbow*. The professor paired these books up, as far as I could tell, for their unreadability.

The professor's name was Ponder. Dr. David L. Ponder. He lived up to his name. Ponder pondered. He ruminated. He mulled. I recently attended a drone music event where about fifteen people played the same cluster of notes at the same time. That's how I would describe attending "Melville and Pynchon" on Monday and Wednesday mornings.

"From the heads of all ponderous profound beings," Ishmael pronounces in *Moby-Dick*, "there always goes up a certain semi-visible steam." I saw no steam as I contemplated the whiteness of Ponder's tennis sneakers, his wrinkled, tan suit, his hands shaking from nicotine-cravings.

• • •

My own look in these years was supposed to signify profundity and danger, but instead resembled a stereotypical lesbian of a certain age: short hockey mullet, black biker jacket, white turtleneck, bright cardigan with tortoise-shell buttons, cuffed blue jeans, Doc Martens, and Morrissey glasses.

Ponder's register remained in bass clef as he lectured on the portentous hermeneutics of white whales, week upon week.

I liked Dr. Ponder. I registered for the class because I heard he was the most brilliant professor in the Rutgers-Camden English Department. I liked him because he smoked.

♦ ♦ ♦

For me, more than anything else, the class was about the struggle to sustain attention. I got high beforehand to make it through 90 minutes of Ponder's ponderings. I took notes as he ground Ahab's wooden leg into ontological-epistemological dust. I doodled while Ponder pulverized Cetology, Leviathans, and noble savages.

Half the class didn't read either book past page 100. These, I must point out, were the goody-good English majors at Rutgers-Camden. They knew that reading the books cover to cover was a waste of time that would be better spent writing papers hewn exactly to Ponder's taste.

♦ ♦ ♦

Soon the class turned into my own great white whale, the object of a monomaniacal mind. Reader, if you have ever studied Melville's book, you could have guessed the observation I made around mid-semester from a nautical mile, for it was then that I started seeing the cocks.

Lots of cocks. Penises, phalli. Everywhere.

♦ ♦ ♦

Was it Melville's mentions of *harpoons* and *long darts* that sealed the deal? Or was it the *omnitooled manmakers* and *pitch-poolers*, *sperm* and *prods* and *grandissimuses*? Or perhaps it was the elastic gunwhales springing in and out, page after page.

No, it was all of these things, as well as the chapter where the whales fuck under water. That, and the word *archbishopricks*.

. . .

One day I came across a quote from D.H. Lawrence where he calls *Moby-Dick* "the great American phallus."

This was my breakthrough, my validation, my spout-hole misting! Avast! Avast there!

For the first time, my academic career, unremarkable up to that point, benefitted from my substantial marijuana habit and coincided with one of my real passions: penis jokes.

. . .

On the day we were to propose paper topics, Ponder ran out the clock holding court with the grad students who audited the class. They sat in the front row exchanging witticisms in thick academic patois, beginning every statement with phrases like "to be sure" or "this passage posits."

"Excuse me, Dr. Ponder," I said, hand raised, interrupting in-joke giggles. "Isn't it possible that the whale isn't some mysterious stand-in for knowledge, but instead represents the *vagina dentata*?"

Ponder grimaced. Was it my mention of *vagina*?

"Maybe Ahab is on a quest to take revenge on the whale, his castrating mother, and calls on the men aboard the Pequod to avenge the loss of his leg, which is really his penis?"

Never mind that castration means cutting your balls off, not your penis, and Ahab's wooden leg would then be a penis replacement. I thought I was brilliant. Dr. Ponder sniggered, coughed, said "well, yes," and then got back to mulling.

"If I could read just one quote," I continued. "It's from the 'Cetology' chapter." I paused as students turned to the page in their Dell Classics editions. Ponder's hands shook in a palsy as he jonesed for tobacco.

245

"Here is it is: 'To grope down into the bottom of the sea after them; to have one's hands among the unspeakable foundations, ribs, and very pelvis of the world; this is a fearful thing.' " I closed my book. "Don't you think the argument can be made that this is Melville's phallic fantasia?"

The period ended. Ponder bolted out and headed for the foyer, Dunhills and lighter in hand.

• • •

I suspected that, like most professors, Ponder thought I was an idiot. I wanted him to think I was smart or at least not dumb. I wanted to prove to him that I possessed a single, original idea. I went to the library and checked out twenty books of Melville criticism, a three-volume *Moby-Dick* concordance, and some interlibrary-loaned articles of great obscurity.

For weeks, I obsessed over books with unusual vigor, writing copious notes on little index cards. I felt like a future public intellectual as I recited *Moby-Dick*'s most cock-filled passages to my roommate, Derek, by this time Rutgers-Camden's biggest pot dealer, in between hits from his electric bong, handcrafted from an aquarium filter and a rubber hose. The Death Bong, made from two goldfish bowls, was powered by an aquarium filter and resembled a hookah. Switched on, Derek's Death Bong issued foghorn sounds that shook our shared wall. Whoever put their mouth on the tube would pass out on his floor as Jane's Addiction played.

• • •

I called my paper "Moby-Cock: Phallicisms in Melville's *Moby-Dick*." Only one handwritten page remains in my files.

"To travel the Pequod with Herman Melville," I began, "is to embark on an exclusively male journey. To extract phallicisms from *Moby-Dick* is to simply draw upon an already existent masculinity and reinforce it. The phallus, erect and flaccid, attached and unattached, appears in many implied and hyperbolic forms in *Moby-Dick*; the archetypal male symbol appears not so much as a motif, but as a fundamental mark in a classic search for manhood."

In the lounge of Armitage Hall, I showed off the final draft to a graduate student. She had long, straight hair, and looked like Sharon Tate. She seemed impressed, or at least acted that way.

◆ ◆ ◆

I received a C- for "Moby-Cock"—a "gentleman's C," as Ponder called it in his comments. He didn't write much. One note mentioned how I lost track of my points and trailed off mid-sentence. He drank bourbon when he marked papers, someone told me.

I deserved the grade. The writing, I'm sure, was horrible, mechanically and on a thought level, as I would put it now, in the professor trade. And I can't help but wonder how I would have graded the paper myself. Would have I have encouraged a "Moby-Cock" paper topic? I mean, when we got to the part where Stubb, the second mate, dons the skin of a whale's penis and conducts some pagan ceremony, would I have said, "My dear boy, sometimes a whale foreskin is just a whale foreskin"?

◆ ◆ ◆

It would be twelve years until I saw David Ponder again. By then I was out of graduate school and living in Williamsburg. I met up with my college friend Trevor, who was screening a film he'd directed at Anthology Film Archives. It had just won the Slamdance Festival. Its plot involves a junkie who cross-dresses to get smack.

There, sitting at the table with Trevor in a Russian bar in the East Village, was a frail man in a light-colored suit and white sneakers. Ponder had given Trevor money for the film, which earned him the illustrious title of associate producer. We drank vodka shots and talked about good old Rutgers-Camden, Henry James, and modern poetry. By this time I had learned that Ponder was, in fact, gay, that he loved cats, and his boyfriend's name was "Titty." I didn't bring up "Moby-Cock," since I doubted that he would remember me.

But he did.

"I enjoyed your comments in class," Ponder said as he out-drank me two shots to one. "Particularly about the Melville. I could tell you were a writer."

I blushed. Such encouragement a decade after the fact had me floating across Second Avenue.

◆ ◆ ◆

What else do I remember about that night? I remember that Ponder cussed like a sailor, that when it was time to go, I said, "Let us go then, you and I," and Ponder recited the rest of Eliot's "Prufrock" from memory. I remember that he held my arm as we crossed Second Avenue, that I helped him with his coat as he took his seat, and that, when the movie started and the white projector beam hit his face just so, he grinned proudly—a grin he held until the final credits.

84.

Notes on Kieron

When I think about Kieron, fellow English major, night owl photographer who spent hours in darkrooms, dipping and hanging prints on clothespins, I think of images, mental snapshots. The first: 1987, a meeting for the college newspaper. Kieron stands in the back with a camera strapped around his forearm. He has long, stringy hair, like the lead singer of Marillion.

• • •

If I try hard, I can conjure the smirk he made as we joked about our student events board's plan to book Dave Wopat, the musician brother of *Dukes of Hazard* actor Tom Wopat, as our spring concert headliner. We pitched stories that railed against student apathy, clueless business majors, jocks who paraded around campus in webbed leather sandals, the evils of Ronald Reagan.

• • •

I had met Aura, Kieron's younger sister, in what passes as Rutgers-Camden's campus green. She was sketching manhole covers. I spent the afternoon in their apartment in the Helene Building, a small castle at the corner of Third and Cooper Streets. At first I was intimidated by Aura and Kieron, whose father was a music professor (and the only faculty member who lived on campus). How easily they spoke about art and writing and music!

Aura was earnest and beautiful with a hearty laugh, but it was Kieron who was the kindred soul.

His flannel shirts, his long black coat and unlaced boots, friendship bracelets and black rubber bands around his wrists.

His voice, easily imitated, nasal and bright, like a confident Napoleon Dynamite.

I can now remember how much I wanted to be like him.

• • •

We spent winter break drinking wine, playing Leonard Cohen, Prince, Flipper, Dead Milkmen. Kieron's taste in music was welcoming, even corny: Steely Dan, Japan, John Prine, Fishbone, Joy Division's "She's Lost Control" 12-inch, Be-Bop Deluxe, Native Tribe hip-hop.

One night we scored free tickets to see Metallica at a small club in Delaware called The Stone Balloon. Kieron and I ran out, our faces bruised and bloodied from moshers' elbows, pants soaked in sweat.

Another night in summer, we cooled off on a rooftop and discussed Diane Arbus, Susan Sontag, and Allen Ginsberg.

• • •

If I could pin down one moment when I first felt a real kinship with Kieron, it would be the night when we went to a party on Point Street, where ten or so long-haired dudes zoned out to Headbangers Ball on MTV. We were there to get pot, or at least to get high.

No one had girlfriends at Rutgers-Camden. Men outnumbered women ten to one, and campus life took on the qualities of a submarine at sea. Someone put on a porno on VHS cassette. I thought Kieron would want to leave or express disgust. Instead, he was curious.

"Don't you think this is kind of strange?" he said.

"What do you mean?" I was embarrassed being in the room. I still wanted to impress him.

Kieron giggled and took another toke. "Why are there fifteen men in a room watching a porn flick together? Are they all just going to go back to their room and jerk off? This is the most homoerotic thing I've ever seen."

I shushed him. Kieron, a super-chatty stoner, was prone to talking for hours in essayistic, serial monologues.

• • •

Eventually, I moved into Kieron's apartment. We became, it is fair to say, best friends. It might be cruel to say I outgrew Scot Harter in Maple Shade or Derek or the metalheads of Point Street, but how else to explain when one group of friends is relegated to the second team—the B-list benchwarmers—of a social life? It's natural for a young person to move from clique to clique and shed one identity for the other, but back then it seemed like I had, in some way, joined the grown-ups. I moved from an apartment with Rutgers-Camden's most successful pot dealer and a mechanized bong to one with vegetable stencil patterns along the walls, yellowed museum posters, and two birds that chirped in the living room.

• • •

William Wordsworth writes about returning to Tintern Abbey, where he recalls the "coarser pleasure of my boyish days." I look at photos of myself from this time—almost always a drink or joint in hand, bleary-eyed, a middle finger stuck out—and try not to think about being young or stupid or naïve. I try not to think about being angry, cynical, or purposefully obnoxious.

To Kieron at times I must have seemed to be some Cro-Magnon. He would have friends over who went to his summer camp, people from the Upper West Side and Westchester, and I stewed with salt-of-the-earth anger at their mannered ways, scoffed at their fear of walking down the streets of Camden. I wasn't fun company.

"I cannot paint / What I then was," Wordsworth writes. Remembering those versions of myself years ago fills me with some nostalgia, but mostly I turn away.

. . .

If these Notes seem like a eulogy, it's because, as I write this, Kieron's been dead more than 10 years. I missed the funeral, which seemed the worst sin I could commit after we lost touch. It happened before Facebook. I didn't find out in time. No one told me, either. I had the basic desire to be with others who knew and loved him, to share in grief with some and to console others.

. . .

I talked to others who went to the funeral. A boombox played Gordon Lightfoot's "The Wreck of the Edmund Fitzgerald," an homage to the scene in *High Fidelity* in which Jack Black's character lists "Top 5 Songs About Death."

I smiled. How we made lists constantly, hanging out in a dead city. We were happy to sit around and laugh at the absurdity of the adulthoods we were about to endure, or talk about a painting or a photograph, or the way a particular guitar sounded on a particular record.

We spent days debating the merits of Peter Greenaway's elaborate tracking shots, rearranging reputations of novelists, poets, directors.

With Kieron, I didn't feel as angry. It never occurred to me that Kieron, or anyone else for that matter, might have been angry as well.

85.

Notes on an Ex-Girlfriend

I met Deena at the start of my senior year. I worked as an orientation group leader, and she sat in the front row, pastel sweater over her hips, white leggings, flats. Deena was pretty in the way some gay men find women pretty, which is to say she had a masculine aspect, over which she put layers of girlyness: gobs of makeup, big red hair. She raised her hand before I even spoke.

"Hey, senior boy, where are the parties?" she asked.

◆ ◆ ◆

We hooked up that Friday at a kegger. At first, I didn't think it was going to be a *girlfriend thing*. My friends didn't think so, either. In a move that was out of character, Kieron offered me relationship advice: Don't get too serious with this new girl.

"I just don't want you to get caught up with somebody who's stupid," Kieron said. "You're better than that."

◆ ◆ ◆

In the Wild Ex-Girlfriend Olympics, Deena would at least earn the bronze. Deena drank so much at parties that I'd pick her up in a fireman's hold, put her into her car, and see her off as a friend drove her home. She drank in the afternoons, in the mornings. She laughed so loud you'd hear it from inside a bar. She never bought drinks. Once, Deena drove on the shoulder of the Garden State Parkway, bypassing a traffic jam, and pulled straight up to a Trooper. She did not get a ticket. Another time she was caught by the police riding the hood of a car on an off-ramp, in a bikini. She did not get a ticket.

. ♦ .

I would describe the time I spent with Deena as one long scowl across the room. It eventually made its way to my side of the room and turned into strikes across my face and then became makeup sex. I am pretty sure she fell in love with me at some point, but I couldn't point to any exact moment that would prove it. We had fun so long as we were drinking or getting high or playing music or fucking.

. ♦ .

Back then, friends would tell me how horrible she was, how loud and obnoxious she was.

But I'm loud and obnoxious, I'd say to them.

86.

Notes on the Pistol

February 27, 1989. I celebrated my twenty-first birthday on the roof of my building with Aura, Kieron, and Derek. We were laughing and making birdcalls down to the street. The Ben Franklin Bridge did its whole throbbing-blue-and-white-streaks thing. We'd taken mushrooms. Each wall we leaned on wobbled; each breeze steadied our feet on the tar.

When we got back to our building, a green "Missed Delivery" slip had been taped to our mailbox by the building manager.

• • •

Kieron and I walked to the post office the next morning. I picked up a brown box from Tucson, Arizona. With its thick brown paper and duct tape, looked like something from Wile E. Coyote's workshop. I tore it open at the counter where people apply for passports and looked inside.

The few times my father remembered my birthday, he sent a dream catcher or a sandstone lizard. Here's what I got this time: a gun. A Jennings 22-caliber semiautomatic pistol. Beside it was a plastic box with fifty rounds of segmented hollow-point bullets. Dad also sent a birthday card.

> Dear Danny:
>
> No white person living in Camden should be unarmed. If you should use this, God forbid, to defend yourself, throw it in the

river, call me collect and I'll send you a
new one.

Love,
Dad

• • •

This is the part where I point out that the Market Street post office also houses the Camden Federal Building and the U.S. Third Circuit Court. I mention this because it seemed best to leave the building in a hurry with my new, unregistered weapon, especially after two gold-tipped cop killer bullets fell out of their box and went *tink-tink-tink* on the marble floor. Kieron and I ran out, falling over each other, like some scene in the Three Stooges.

• • •

It didn't occur to me then that my father might be crazy. That would come a couple years later. I was too busy laughing. Getting a pistol in the mail was funny, you see. Not funny ha-ha; more funny what-the-fuck. Or maybe I convinced myself of this. Or maybe it was proof that my father was dangerous or unpredictable, and by extension I was as well.

• • •

Kieron and I performed T.J. Hooker rolls on the couch and *To Live and Die In L.A.* squats. We held the gun in the air with a John Woo-style sideways grip.

• • •

On the phone weeks later, Dad said he regretted sending me a gun in the mail. "I just wanted to give you something permanent," he said. "It was probably a stupid thing to do."

・　・　・

My time as an illegal handgun owner ended when, after drinking several glasses of grain alcohol punch and arguing with Deena, I threatened to kill myself in front of her, in the clumsy way troubled, lovesick college kids do, and stuck the barrel in my mouth. It had no bullets. I turned it in on one of those no-questions-asked days at the Camden Police Department.

・　・　・

I wrote about Dad's birthday present for a personal essay class. I called it "The Gun and the Damage Done." Here's the first paragraph:

> Even the most crazy, twisted and whacked-out gun freaks observe a kind of protocol, wherein they wouldn't do foolish and potentially life-threatening things with their weapons. They would not, for in-stance, point an unloaded cocked gun at a sleeping person's forehead, waking them up with the pull of a trigger. But that's exactly the kind of hijinks that happened when I got my hands on a pistol in 1989.

I was reading a lot of Hunter S. Thompson, in case that isn't obvious.

・　・　・

"The Gun and the Damage Done" was entered into the Rutgers Spring Writers Conference workshop led by a sports writer we'll call Chestpuff McNutsack. Five people had their work selected to be critiqued. I thought it was an honor to be selected.

I sat in the back of the science building auditorium and lis-tened to Chestpuff McNutsack tear the essay apart. There was the "latent homoeroticism" of the gun, he said, combined with "the worst kind of male braggadocio." The sixty people in the auditorium laughed and cringed. Several raised their hands to comment on how correct Chestpuff McNutsack's comments were.

I didn't admit to writing it. I sat in the back seat, chuckling.

• • •

Now that I am a teacher myself, I would like to say that his critique ended up being good for me, that the feedback rattled me to correct and adjust immature habits of mind. It wasn't the first instance of public discouragement I'd received about my writing—that same weekend, a poetry teacher said my writing "hung like wet laundry on the line."

What I did have back then was naïve ambition, which helped brush off any hurt by lunchtime. It's a quality I wish I still had, rather than a chronic anger, another gift from my father, one that I fear is permanent.

87.

Notes on a
Legal Settlement

Four years, several depositions, and two canceled court dates later, the ponytailed lawyer and I settled with the lawnmower company for damages owed for my Achilles tendon. I never knew there was a Blue Book for a human body that sets monetary amounts for each part. My right ankle was ruled as 10% out of commission.

Using that figure as a reference, along with pain and suffering and the shitty way the company put together their lawn movers, I got $120,000. Minus the lawyer's 33% contingency fee and paying back the hospital, I cleared $41,000.

· · ·

It might not sound like a fortune, but if it wasn't for that $41,000, I have no doubt that I would have turned out differently. I'd be back working at some car wash on the White Horse Pike or hammering away at some mundane task in a cubicle. For some reason I envision this alternate version of myself behind the counter at an Enterprise Rent-a-Car.

The money bought time, time to write horrible poems, time to read books, time to smoke pot. Without it, I wouldn't have graduated from college. Without it, I wouldn't be the mid-list professor-slash-writer I am today.

· · ·

The day came for the first big installment, the first $10,000. Derek drove me to the lawyer's office and offered me three pieces of advice.

"First, give me three thousand of it so I can buy a whole lot of pot to sell," he said. "I'll pay you back in a month with 25% interest."

"Second, don't get into coke. And third," Derek grabbed my chin and made me look straight into his eyes, "whatever you do, don't buy Deena an engagement ring."

I didn't know what he meant. We'd been broken up for almost a year by then.

· · ·

And then, like magic, Deena reappeared. We even moved in together, sharing a house in Collingswood, a sleepy town near my old high school, with a mutual stoner friend. Before I knew it, I was hemorrhaging hundreds a month, paying everyone's rent, food, appliances.

"You have *all that money*," she said, hitting me up for a thousand bucks for her mom's new transmission.

· · ·

We made it four months under the same roof. I'll skip over the domestic tedium that led to the household's collapse, an experience I have described before as resembling a community theater production of *Who's Afraid of Virginia Woolf?* Toward the end of *our living in sin*, as my mother called it, I took over my Uncle Frank's paper route while he was on vacation. I got up at five o'clock in the morning, but Deena desired not to be roused at such an ungodly hour. I slept in our skanky basement.

Maybe the alarm clock that fell on my head knocked sense into me. One morning, I drove over to Philly after my route and walked into TLA Video to look at apartment postings. The first one I saw, a one-bedroom on Spruce Street, looked promising enough. I took the whole flyer down so no one else could see it.

. . .

It happened so quickly—the pay phone call, the meeting with a guy my age with gelled-back hair and a crème-colored BMW, him opening the door to show me a 300-square-foot apartment with a two-burner stove. It had tall windows and was close to my two favorite bars: McGlinchey's and Dirty Frank's.

I signed the lease on the wall of the kitchen and started to move out while Deena was at work. Before I could make my second trip, the rest of my stuff was out on the curb.

88.

Notes on Autobiography: Asides (Delicate and Unique)

The act of writing autobiography, Roy Pascal writes in *Design and Truth in Autobiography*, "postulates a pre-occupation with the self that may, and often does, deteriorate into vanity, complacency, self-indulgence."

The best autobiographies, he says, balance the subjective self and the objective world, "inspired by a reverence for the self, tender yet severe, that sees the self not as property but a trust."

$\cdot \quad \cdot \quad \cdot$

I would like to believe that by keeping in mind as I examine myself that I am a vessel and not the source of whatever wisdom I may come up with, I avoid vanity and self-indulgence. But there's another side of me that is vain, that does aspire to self-indulgence. How dare I, after all, express my self's "delicate uniqueness," as if my story should be heard above everyone else's?

$\cdot \quad \cdot \quad \cdot$

I want to let the gears show in these Notes, to not present myself with a complacence I see with so much other writing, including some of my own. I want to remember that no one can get an experience down just right. I want, in the end, to be delicate and unique.

89.

Notes on Dad's Year Off:
Prologue

Flashback to eighth grade: I had approached Dad as he sat in his chair. His afternoons were no longer filled with Gregorian chants and Carlos Castaneda books, but by smoking beside a silent phone, waiting for work to call.

"Did you really skip the second grade because you were too smart?"

"Yep," he said.

"How did it happen?"

"It was a new school, so it was easier to jump a grade. No one knew who I was anyway. My parents were very proud."

◆ ◆ ◆

This is what I knew: Mom and Dad were born a few days apart in June 1947. Both started high school the same year, and both were members of the graduating class of 1965, Dad from Bisbee High and Mom from Merchantville High.

"So, if you and Mom are the same age," I continued, "and Mom didn't skip a grade, why did you both graduate from high school in the same year? Shouldn't you have graduated the year before?"

Dad took a drag, issued jets of smoke out of his nostrils, surprised that his son was capable of basic math.

"All you need to know," he said, "is that I took junior year off."

When did I first hear the real story of Dad's "year off"?

"He ran into a lot of trouble when he was a kid," was how Uncle Frank put it at a cookout. We were shooting marbles with a wrist rocket slingshot into a watermelon across the yard. "Every boy does."

. . .

My grandparents' divorce was not as tidy as it was described when I was younger. Elena, Michael's older sister, married a college kid and moved to Bisbee, a border town 80 miles south of Tucson. This left Michael alone with quarreling, unstable parents. Dr. Murlin Nester, the distant husband, had "dalliances with nurses." Mary Ellen Nester used her husband's prescription pad to get drugs. Over the course of junior high, according to my mother, Michael would come home to find his mother, by then a full-fledged addict, in bed with a succession of men. When the marriage of Murlin and Mary Ellen finally did dissolve, Dr. Nester "burnt the family home to the ground."

Mary Ellen Nester moved to Ohio. Dr. Nester dispatched his 15-year-old son to live in a trailer by himself. He gave him his own credit card.

. . .

Mike Nester took scooter trips to Nogales. I knew Dad had a scooter; it's part of the reason I wanted to get a moped, to be more like him. What I didn't know until later is what happened on these Nogales trips.

"The time he spent living in a trailer was one big party," is how Mom put it years later. "He hung out with bad companions and consorted with loose women." He drove a scooter out to Monterey. On Cannery Row, he got the tattoo on his right arm: a U.S. coat of arms, *e pluribis unum* and an eagle clutching an olive branch and arrows.

One of his friends "knocked over a California gas station."
It's unclear if Dad acted as an accomplice or a main player. "I do
know they shot a couple dogs along the way," my mother said.
"And he knew a guy who shot an Indian."

· ◆ ·

The stories differ over why my father was arrested. Blowing
up pipe bombs was what got him in trouble. That or after he
bought a six-pack. Whichever way, when Dad was 16, he was arrested, processed through the offices of Waldon V. Burr, longtime
sheriff of Pima County. The one time Dad spoke of the sheriff, he
described him as a "corrupt son of a bitch."[20]

He then spent his junior year, 1963–1964, in The Arizona
Industrial School for Wayward Boys and Girls at Fort Grant,
part of the Arizona Department of Corrections. By 1964, Fort
Grant had developed a reputation as the toughest juvenile de-
tention center in the country, a segregated facility with separate
dorms for whites, blacks, Native Americans, and Hispanics. A
1952 *Time* magazine report mentions "whippings, blackjack-
ings, and assorted cruelties" on the inmates, referred to as boys.
Superintendent Gary R. Ridge confessed in testimony that he
used corporal punishment on his inmates.

"But none of the boys that I know of limped after they were
whipped," he said in his defense.[21]

---

20 Aside: the 1964 *Rawhide* episode "Incident of the Rusty Shotgun" features a villain called Sheriff Burr, played by actor Herbert Anderson, fresh from playing
the father on *Dennis the Menace*. Another: in 1968, Sheriff Waldon Vivian Burr
was indicted on 80 counts for, in part, soliciting bribes from deputies.

21 In the same *Time* story: description of how the FBI investigated an incident of a
12-year-old runaway who had been "clubbed, whipped, hung by the neck until
almost strangled, then hauled down and finally forced at whip's-end to run in
front of a truck until he collapsed." And these were the white inmates.

· · ·

Let's call it situational irony that, just when I was trying to make myself out to be an outlaw badass motherfucker, I find out my father was more outlaw, more of a badass motherfucker than I could ever be.

Notes on the Last Arizona Trip

On New Year's Eve, 1990, I stood on top of the Berlin Wall, and saw both the East and West sides. Kieron and I took a trip there when the Wall fell. A photographer for *Stars and Stripes* mistook Kieron and Aura and me for German college students and took a photo of us. "They danced, they sang, and drank champagne," the caption reads. I saw Michael Hasselhoff sing wearing a jacket studded with L.E.D. lights atop a crane.

A couple weeks later on a plane to Arizona, I brought a couple pebbles I'd chipped away myself.

• • •

It was a short visit. Dad seemed nervous the whole time. Over shots of tequila in Nogales, we got the closest we'd ever had to a complete, adult conversation. Dad told me how he escaped "juvie jail," as he called it, and hitchhiked to Tennessee, where his mother's side of the family lived. He worked at a gas station under an assumed name and tried to enlist in the Navy, but he couldn't. He was a 16-year-old escapee without a high school diploma. Finally, one day, he called the warden at Fort Grant. "It's me," he said, "and I'm coming back."

He hopped on a bus back to Arizona, served out the end of his time, and moved to Bisbee the next year to finish high school, where he was put under the guardianship of his sister.

· · ·

Instead of donning a cap and gown, Mike Nester walked straight to the military recruitment center in downtown Bisbee and enlisted in the Navy. After basic training, he signed up to be stationed anywhere: Operation Deep Freeze in Antarctica; Berlin, Germany; the island of Diego Garcia in the Indian Ocean. At the top of his list was a request to be part of U.S. action in Vietnam, where the number of deployed military personnel had jumped from 17,280 in 1964 to 129,611 in 1965 and 317,007 in 1966. He was turned down for all of these assignments because of his juvenile record. Instead, he was stationed in Philadelphia.

Mike Nester, a sailor who never went to sea.

· · ·

The night before I left, we ate dinner at my Aunt Elena's. My father always looked like a caged animal in his more prosperous sister's house. I followed him outside by the pool for one of his many cigarette breaks. He was hacking up deep, emphysemic coughs that echoed against the adobe walls.

"You should stop smoking," I said. "It'll kill you."

He ashed in a cactus pot, then got right in my face.

"Don't you ever tell me what to fucking do," he said. His eyes seemed crazy. He looked at me for a second, then stepped back.

· · ·

We drove to the airport the next morning. Early in the visit it felt like we had reached some rapprochement, détente. Whatever French word you want to use for getting closer, it went away that last night. I felt like, as people used to say, *my own man.*

Just like the old days, when we got in the car, we fought over which radio station to tune to. He stopped at a gas station. He climbed out of the car to get a pack of smokes. I stayed inside, pushed the thick preset buttons that slid up and down the frequency dial.

George Michael's "Father Figure" started to play. The record snob in me knew I should switch the station. But I kept it on. As the breathy vocals started, I studied my father outside, watched him walk toward the convenience store, his duck feet gait in work boots, how he flirted with the cashier.

I noticed all this—how he packed his box of Marlboro Reds, the way he placed the pack in the pocket of his Mexican shirt. These are the habits we hold on to. He lit a cigarette outside the door. Three-shake wave of the match, then a toss.

And I started to cry. I was going to miss him. I missed him already. I had always missed him. I felt sorry for him and I loved him at the same time. I could feel his body rise out of mine. I could feel my childhood come back with each move of his that I recognized.

I see my small children now, how they look at me, how they absorb everything. They're sponges. They're taking notes and asking questions already.

•   •   •

He pumped the gas. He looked away from the truck, toward the mountains. I thought then that he did this so he did not have to think how he would say goodbye to his son.

The song continued. I cried some more. I was leaving him in the desert, and I hated my life back home. I didn't know where I was going. I was 21 and still a child, an angry child.

Most of what he gave me only hurt. I knew then I couldn't be mad all my life, but on that day, I was sad and angry and in love with him as much as any son could be.

The song ended. For the first time of my visit, I turned off the music. For the first time of my visit, I took out a cigarette from his open pack and lit it. We drove off of the gas station island, both with our sunglasses on, both blowing smoke out of our windows.

I never saw my father again.

91.

Notes on Mentors

Can a mentor relationship exist unawares to both mentor and mentee? In a mentorship, advice is passed down, and what I am about to discuss involves two parties, two poets, one a master and another an apprentice. Does it have to be called a mentorship while it's happening?

· · ·

I look back with regret at mentorships I could have enjoyed, if only I had been more open to having them. Witnessing a real, live mentorship while growing up helps you understand that it can happen to you as well. Although I have had many excellent teachers in my lifetime, I never thought I could call one a mentor. I was wrong.

· · ·

In September 1991, I took my first poetry workshop, led by Walt Booker. I paid for it in cash with my ankle settlement. I was a nonmatriculated student studying in the same English department I'd tormented for five years as an undergraduate. Our class met in the special collections room in the Rutgers-Camden Paul Robeson Library, around a large wooden table surrounded by glass-enclosed shelves that held books and documents significant to South Jersey's rich history.[22]

---

22 As a stand-up comedian once deadpanned onstage in the student center lounge, "you can just feel the history seeping through the cinderblocks."

• • •

Sitting there, I felt like I had made it to The Show. I was champing at the bit to write poems, real poems: not apprentice work or mere exercises for class but poems for the ages. I read T.S. Eliot's "Tradition and the Individual Talent" on a monthly basis, pondering over statements like "The emotion of art is impersonal" and how tradition was important "to anyone who would continue to be a poet beyond his twenty-fifth year," an age I was approaching.[23] The papers I wrote for this class, cringeworthy in their dudgeon and formality, were supposed to cover "prosody," and even though I had looked the term up, I hardly mentioned the "science and study of poetic meters and versification," choosing to focus instead on My Struggle to Find My Own Voice.

• • •

Twenty-three students met every Tuesday, huge for a graduate class. I wanted to be the star. I was a 22-year-old English grad and felt like I was running out of time.

• • •

Booker was the first professor who offered a model for how a "blue collar" person could become a writer. He was 38, had worked in a factory in Baltimore for more than 10 years before moving on in the world of writing. By the slowness of his gait, I could tell he'd lifted things, moved large things around. My father's shoulders, my grandpop's shoulders, rounded down like his. There's a certain way people who work on their feet and do

---

23 I see now that Eliot was doing some pretty entry-level straw men shit, right from the beginning. "In English writing we seldom speak of tradition," he writes, "though we occasionally apply its name in deploring its absence." Of course now I can question whether we ever seldom spoke of tradition, but since T.S. Fucking Eliot was saying it, I took it all as Bible truth.

physical labor sit in a chair: back straight up, legs uncrossed and close together, feet planted on the floor. I still sit that way, years away from mopping and washing cars. Booker sat that way, too. Tall and black, Booker would walk into the room and rarely move from his chair until the class was over. I hung on his every word.

• • •

It was a workshop, the kind where you make copies of your poems and exchange them with the class, but it wasn't just about that. Booker made us read. A lot. We bought twenty books that semester: Keats and Whitman and Dickinson, Lucille Clifton, Sharon Olds, C.K. Williams, Garrett Hongo, Li-Young Lee, Philip Levine. And then there were Booker's own poems, trenchant and elegiac with an obvious and brave sadness.

• • •

That semester, I wrote 5–6 poems a week, a rate that I can only dream of now, and sat in Booker's class filled with a fire I can also only dream of now. The poems were all terrible. I did, however, know how to give things titles, probably since most of my reading came off record sleeves: "Eliot's Religion & A New Way to Screw," "Complicated Bar Elegy," "The Aesthetics of the Pennsauken Mart," "I Always Fall in Love with Waitresses."

• • •

Toward the end of the semester, we sat down in his office and, in his deep voice, Booker asked me a question that changed the course of my life.

"Well Dan," he said, looking at a stack of poems, "what are you going to do with all these poems?"

· · ·

There are too many epiphanies, the forced products of editors and book doctors keen to make writing come to some sudden flare of meaning. Real epiphanies are reconstructions, reenactments of the wisdom we arrive at. Far from cheapening that wisdom, the tale of an epiphany, however small, shares with readers the process, the getting-there, which is often as important as the epiphany itself.

These Notes reenact this epiphany: that I could matter, that I could write, that there was a world outside my world.

· · ·

A mentor does more than validate a student's work, to be sure, but with this question, Booker became mine. Before I could process all this, we talked about this thing called graduate school, where you can get a degree in creative writing. In poetry! I'd never heard of such a thing. The idea seemed ridiculous to me, at least at first. Ridiculous and glorious, I mean. It also seemed too good to be true.

At the time, however, I resisted. I said that I wanted to live out in the real world, whatever the hell that meant. Can I go back and slap myself?

"Well Dan, you could keep writing poems and see what Beer Guzzler Joe at the bar has to say," Booker said. "Or you could find other poets and study with someone whose work you respect."

We talked about New York City. "You can always find a street corner," he said, "where people will clap for whatever you're doing." People would clap? For me?

· · ·

Let's be honest: although Walt Booker and I shared a lot—poetry and work, a love for free jazz and Robert Hayden's "Those

Winter Sundays"—we were different people. And to expect a mentor requires no small amount of entitlement, and if there was anything I didn't have in my twenties, it was feeling entitled to anything. In young adulthood, the full effect of one's background still asserts itself, and I was taught to expect less so that nothing disappointed.

Lots of people disappointed me back then. Booker was not one of them.

• • •

Even among peers and professors whose work I loved, I brought with me, as Phillip Lopate once called it, a "working class mistrust of the university environment." So I found myself in this middle ground at all times, feeling slighted on the one hand but also lucky to be in the same room as my esteemed faculty and fellow students.

I expected to be rejected, or to reject him, and that would be the end of our relationship. Neither happened. He just helped me, validated me, and sent me along my way. Is that mentorship? I hope it is. Whichever the case, what I have learned is that it's best to acknowledge one's mentors, and, two decades later, that's better than not doing anything at all. I look back at times with a terrible regret for not being more open to having mentors or acknowledging them. I think of Walt Booker now as a mentor, one of only a few, but that's all you need in a lifetime.

92.

Notes on Siblings

"Did you hear?" Meri said on the phone. "Dad has a kid!"

"What? I didn't even know he had a girlfriend."

"It's Leanne," Meri said. "You know—the other woman. They got back together. They have a kid!"

I was still processing. "How did you find out?"

"He called. Last night. We have a half sister now, Daisy Mae Nester. Eight pounds, eight ounces. He's sending pictures."

He never came home to visit these past five years, the last birthday present he sent me was a 22-caliber pistol, and now Dad was taking another crack at parenting?

. . .

A week or so later, we looked at the pictures. Dad, shirtless and hairy, hoists Daisy Mae over his shoulders, half smiling. The baby girl was beautiful, with chubby legs and bright eyes. My sister and I kept the baby secret from Mom for about a year, until one day we both told her as we sat on the beach.

"Well," she said, "I guess it was the gentlemanly thing to do."

. . .

Years later, I deep-Googled Daisy Mae Nester and her younger brother, Chuck Nester, my long-lost half siblings. The only web search result I got was a story of when Daisy Mae was a 9-year-old, practicing guitar.

"Another student at Fandango, Daisy Mae Nester, also enjoys playing the guitar. She tells me, 'When I'm feeling sad I play a happy song and then I feel happy!' "

That "feeling sad" broke my heart. I had heard that Leanne and the kids split from Dad and moved away. The first thing I thought about what made her feel sad, of course, was what we had in common: her father, my father, our father. I thought about her practicing, staying after school, all to avoid going home. How isolated in her own interests, how her hobbies offered escape.

I found Daisy Mae and Chuck on MySpace. They had moved to another state and set their profiles to private, and only Daisy Mae answered my friend request. We exchanged messages. The main thing I wanted to know is whether they turned out OK. It looked like they did: My half sister is indeed a musician and a band geek, bless her heart. I clicked through pictures of her smiling with friends, her boyfriend, and a trip to Disney World.

The half brother had a big square head just like me. He put guns and bullets as his wallpaper on his page. White power music played automatically, and I got a chill up my neck. He'd bought into the militaristic thing way more than I had.

I told Daisy Mae we're expecting our second daughter, and she wanted to know what we're naming her. "I love babies," she said.

Chuck "just hates Dad so much that he doesn't want anything to do with him," she said. "He is trying to change his last name to my mother's maiden name."

They're all scared of him, she said. They have a restraining order on him. I told her I'm scared of him, too, scared of talking to him.

He'd been in and out of alcohol rehab at the VA hospital. In their last days together, my father, drunk and on pills, shot a couple rounds into the mattress. When my half sister asked him why, he says, "It's better than shooting your mother."

"So I'm pretty scared of him, too," she said. "Especially now with missing teeth and a white beard."

. . .

I checked their profiles a couple months later. Both were gone.

93.

Notes on Cousin Mike

My mother has sent me emails over the years expressing her worry about coming off as "looking stupid" in this book. I may not make a good protagonist in this story, but what I do know is my mother is the hero of this one. She's the person who stayed, the person who fought for the roof and filled the fridge.

• • •

My mother remains an open book. For a period of ten years, I sat at her dining room table in Laurel Springs, New Jersey, for our many interviews. We drank coffee with vanilla-flavored creamer as Murphy, an insane beagle, ran around their kitchen. On my recordings, paw-nails make tap dance recital sounds on a faux hardwood floor.

• • •

It's around this time my family started looking at Dad not as my father but as another person entirely: less a person and more of a character. We gave him a name: Cousin Mike. There are so many other Mikes in our family: Big Mike, Little Mike, Mike, Jr.— it was inevitable Mike Nester would turn into someone else.

I traced the nickname back to Meri, which led to a longer conversation with my sister. "It's a coping mechanism from around the time I had children," she said. "My boys don't have a grandfather. I felt a significant void there. I just never wanted to shut off that line of communication. I just downgraded him and lowered my expectations."

• ◆ •

"Considering all his obstacles," she said, "emotionally, he actually did better than one would expect." Years after this conversation, I now see that my sister, my sister of few words and Shader wisdom, was right.

"Did he need to ask you those questions when you were in second grade? No. But when we were in college, it would have been interesting questions to pose. It's like he knew he wouldn't be around when the time came that you would normally ask those existential questions. It's like he was your mental trainer."

I did not want to poke holes in her logic here. The "mental training" my sister speaks of sounds cruel the second it comes out of her mouth, and I can tell from my end of the phone that she thinks the same way. It is as if we figured out how my father's obsessions and teaching came at the same time the grandfather we never met, the demented Dr. Nester, had given his son hormone shots.

• ◆ •

"For the record, I love Dad," my sister said, her voice cracking on my recording. "Not for the shit he did not do, or for the shit I wished he did. I love him for the little piece that he tried to give to us. It was the best he could do, really. He exposed us to things such as art, literature and open freedom of thought that Mom would not have done for us. Even if Dad dabbled in radical views, he had every right to think whatever he wanted to think. He never truly hated anyone, really." Pause. "Except his slutty ex-wife's cat, which he shot."

"I guess I am still wondering how we turned out the way we did," I said.

"You're forgetting we had Mom. She filled in all the cracks and voids as best she could. She had her mom and dad as role models."

"And we have ours."

"And we have ours."

 . . .

June 2007. A few weeks before our first daughter was born, my wife and I go to the ob/gyn for a final ultrasound. Our doctor pours goo and waves a medical wand over my wife's belly in slow motions. We talk about our nervousness over being parents for the first time. The doctor plays jazz saxophone on weekends and has a super-smooth voice that has set us at ease. He tells us about his own daughters, now grown, how distinct they are from each other.

He's as old as my dad, I think. Our daughter starts kicking her feet on the screen. We see her hands, her hair, and her big Nester head.

"For better or worse," our doctor says, as he wipes goo off with a white towel, "parents have a huge influence on how their children see the world."

94.

Notes on Self-Awareness

The last time Dad called Mom was two weeks after her second husband died suddenly. The phone rang. She read ARIZONA NESTER M on Caller ID and still answered.

It must have been the wine she was drinking in the middle of the day or the Ativan that got her courage up. She thought he'd called to offer his sympathies. They hadn't spoken in twenty years.

•　•　•

Dad had heard about Mom's second husband dying, but he called for another reason.

"I thought that you maybe came into a lot of money," he said. "I'm taking early retirement, and I just want to get all my ducks in a row."

He had called to make sure his first wife wouldn't place a claim on his Teamsters pension.

If only he hadn't called.

"I hadn't thought much about it," Mom told him. She'd been busy planning the funeral, writing thank-you cards.

How would she have known he was retiring early in the first place? They hadn't talked in over twenty years. She wanted to let sleeping dogs lie. He knew Patti's second husband had made good money. Before that, Mom never claimed alimony because of her "Irish pride." Now, all these years later, Dad wanted her to promise, right then and there, that she wouldn't ask for her share of his pension.

"I didn't come into any money," she explained. No insurance settlement payout, just a small pension. "But since you never sent support checks to your children for all those years, I'll call my lawyer in the morning."

In case we haven't established my mother is a classy badass lady already, I hope this story accomplishes that.

• • •

You'd think—or I'd think—Mike hung up. But he didn't. They talked for two more hours. She told him he sounded like he lost his sense of humor. He agreed. They talked about Amway, the kerosene heater. They said goodbye.

Then, a couple days later, Dad called my mother again to say, in her words, "How much he misses 'effing' me."

This is the third time I took that quote out and then put it back in. My final decision: It needs to stay.

Notes on Philadelphia, 1991

I wanted to escape to New York, but hiding out in Philly had to do for a while.

♦ ♦ ♦

On the first night in my new apartment, I decided to go out alone into the city. I smoked a joint Derek gave me as a house-warming present and biked down to Old City to the big art house theater to see *Manhattan*. I wanted to see the opening fireworks scene set to Gershwin on the big screen. And when the fireworks started, I realized I had moved to the wrong city.

"Hey, listen, I don't even wanna have this conversation," Diane Keaton's character says. "I'm just from Philadelphia, you know. We believe in God."

♦ ♦ ♦

Philly is comfortable, familial, scolding. I didn't want to be comfortable. "Philadelphia makes short work of a certain kind of ego," Jonathan Franzen writes in an introduction to a book of photos of bar regulars. "It refuses to flatter our sense of self-importance."

♦ ♦ ♦

Poets in Philly talked about the Big Local Prize: $50,000. I noticed how when poets got the Big Local Prize, they promptly left Philly. The dream of the Philly poet, it seemed, was to leave Philly.

. . .

When my very first poem was published, an elegy for Freddie Mercury, it seemed to legitimize what I was doing. Then I was invited to become an editor for a local literary journal. I thought I had made it. Join an editorial board? When do I start?

I was given my first task: a canvas mail bag full of submissions. When it was dropped off my doorstep, I thought it was dirty laundry or stuff Deena had left out on the street. Inside were hundreds of envelopes, plump with manuscripts and self-addressed stamped envelopes and too-clever cover letters. Writers from all over the world sent work: in the first bag were big stars like Ruth Stone and Charles Bukowski, and five envelopes from Lyn Lifshin, aka The Most Published Poet in America. I gathered quickly that we were all in this crazy-kooky poetry business together.

. . .

I wrote Yes, No, or Maybe on the back of the envelopes with a short comment. Sometimes my notes would be short and cruel ("these poems could not suck ass any more") other times magnanimous ("excellent; if we do not take these poems, we should seriously reconsider our mission as a literary concern"). I learned how to articulate which poems I wanted to be published and which ones I thought didn't deserve it. I learned how to find common ground with other editors and figure out my own sensibility. I was surprised to find out I was not unteachable or unmentorable. I could learn.

. . .

For most of the two years I was in Philly, I worked as a proofreader at the Arthur Andersen accounting firm. The job paid 11 dollars an hour, and it gave me time to write poems between checking the math of end-of-year reports and taming consultants' purple prose.

Long before Enron did the company in, Arthur Andersen's offices at 1601 Market Street seemed filled with dread. Graphic designers sat still, shell-shocked over the drudgery of their first jobs after art school. I was, as my supervisor, Dick, called me, "Dan the Temp." I insisted he refer to me as "Dan the Freelancer." He always refused.

Dick saw his main job perk as giving me orders, and when there was nothing to proofread, he would send me into the Xerox Room to punch holes in documents so he could read his Superman comics in peace.

• • •

One day in December, Lena, Dick's supervisor, a nice woman who made my job tolerable, had been unceremoniously fired. The head of Document Production called a meeting that morning, not to wish us a happy holiday, but to say things were *going to be run differently in the new year*. No one knew what that meant, but with Lena gone, I knew Dick would only ramp up his Dick-ish torment of me.

After the meeting, I overheard some office gossip: a young male associate has been outed as gay. This was a big deal at a Philadelphia accounting firm in the early nineties. Everyone gossiped about it like he'd been identified as a leper.

• • •

Dick sent me to the Xerox Room to bind some proposals. All the talk about Lena getting fired and the gay accountant had everyone buzzing, including Karl, the philosopher-griot of the Xerox Room. I liked Karl. Outspoken and crude, he reminded me of my uncles. Karl worked in front of loud machines all his life:

printing presses, mimeographs, hole punchers, top-feed copiers. Because of this, Karl spoke even the most subtle and private comment in *fortissimo* belly-shouts.

"I don't know what the fuss is about the guy being a fag," Karl said as I walked in.

"I mean, one Saturday night, a bunch of my buddies got in my Continental with a case of beer. We picked up this guy by the park, give him a couple beers. He cleaned all our pipes out. It was no big deal."

I went out for lunch and never came back.

• • •

I went to Dirty Frank's that night. Somebody played John Coltrane and Johnny Hartman's version of "Lush Life." I smoked a cigarette outside, looked up at snow coming down. Flakes hit my nose. I had what Virginia Woolf calls a "moment of being," one of those times when a memory is covered in a protective coating, separated from reality.

Notes on Bill's Story

Bill took my mother to the Merchantville High School prom in 1965. She broke up with him before he went off to Vietnam. Mom met Dad shortly after that. Patti and Bill reunited 37 years later in a marriage so romantic and small-town America that it makes me blush. It's one of the many things for which I have Maple Shade to thank.

· · ·

My current stepfather told me once that I should "stop picking on Maple Shade." My mother attributes her third husband's boosterism to his never having worked in town or raised kids there. I explained to him that picking on The Shade is only half the story, that I had to hate the place in order to leave it, and once I did, I stopped hating it and grew to love the place.

When I published a piece about the Mary's Café King story, Bill called me right away. I thought he was upset for mentioning him by name, which I did, or for putting down Maple Shade, which I kind of did as well.

He didn't care about either, which made me love him even more. He'd called to ask me a question.

"That King thing," he began, "did that really happen?"

· · ·

I've been interviewing my mother—at her dining room table or smoking outside, with a tape recorder and without, with a notebook and without—for almost a decade now. I'd ask the same questions and get different answers, or she'd go off on some tangent or take a smoke break out on the porch.

"Drink the pickle juice, hon," she said to my wife, then pregnant with our second daughter. "It helps with your leg cramps."

Through it all, Mom's third husband has sat nearby in his recliner, a chair so comfortable I instantly fall asleep whenever I sat in it. It vibrates and has a refrigerator inside the arms. He would watch SportsCenter and never say a word.

Until one day.

· · ·

"You do know I slept with your father before your mother did, right?"

I turned around to Bill. "What was that you just said?"

"I said that I slept with your dad before your mom did."

I had no explanation for this. "You were gay? My dad was gay?"

"No, ya silly," he said.

And then he told me this story.

· · ·

It was 1966, and Bill was home from Vietnam. "It was snowing outside, coming down in sheets, and I was driving down Main Street. And on the corner of Forklanding, at the bus stop, was a sailor. He looked cold."

"And I drive up and say, 'Looks like the bus ain't comin' anytime soon, sailor. You need a place to stay?' And he gets in the car, and I drive home. I was staying at my mom's house, and she made a bed for him in the top room. He was very nice. He drank some coffee in the morning and made his way back to the bus stop."

The sailor's name? Mike Nester.

. . .

Past The Jade on the hill out of town is a sign, "Welcome to Maple Shade: Nice Town, Friendly People." It reminds me of when I was assigned to read *Our Town* in high school; how, like Thornton Wilder's Grover's Corners, Maple Shade is a town with no scenery, no props, a lot of grief. But like Grover's Corners, there is something eternal about Maple Shade, something that sticks with me wherever I go.

As *Our Town's* Stage Manager says, "Nice town, ya know what I mean?"

97.

Last Notes on The Shade

Whenever I am near Maple Shade's borders, I take a cruise down Main Street. I drive by the custard stand, now open all year, and Main Street Music, shuttered for decades. I cruise down West Woodlawn Avenue to see how the new owners have treated our old house. My sister does this, too: once, she struck up a conversation with the house's current owners, a fireman and his wife, and offered to buy them a new door so she could take home the one inside that still bears marks where we penciled our heights. I look at the playground of Our Lady of Perpetual Help, which used to be a concrete prairie but is now filled with jungle gyms, climbing walls, and a seesaw. I slow down past Inglesby Funeral Home, where hundreds of people came to the viewing of my grandmother.

My wife and daughters have grown tired of these tours of Maple Shade. They beg me to get on the Turnpike to head home.

• • •

There's a guy I know, another Shader Record Nerd, who now lives in Nashville, where he plays country music and wears ten-gallon hats. On Facebook, he wrote to me about how his parents, now in their 80s, have lived in the same house in Maple Shade for 63 years. It was a dirt road when the house was built. He's been coming home to take care of their affairs and wonders what to do when his parents pass on.

"There's a small part of me," he writes, "that wants to keep it as a vacation home, where I can go to hide in my own Maple Shade nostalgia, to remind myself of how I escaped or maybe how it let me escape."

◆ ◆ ◆

A couple years ago, I drove up to the Wawa on Forklanding Road, where Shader motorheads with their monster trucks used to confer in the parking lot. I saw a couple of people hanging out in front with colored mohawks.

Colored mohawks! I had rocks thrown at me because I listened to R.E.M., and these kids were openly embracing funny haircuts and—could it be?—one of them was wearing a Black Flag t-shirt?

◆ ◆ ◆

What I want to point out here: these Notes don't add up to some redemption story of How I Became a Punk Rocker. I never started a zine, never moshed at all-age hardcore shows. I did not grow up to be a sophisticated rock critic. It is just as stupid to listen to ZZ Top all your life as it is to dress some part and hop on the train to go to The Crypt to see GG Allin pee on a skinhead. Scratch any South Jersey punker and you'll find a poseur rich kid from Haddonfield or Montclair.

Shader chicks didn't grow up to be riot grrrls. Shader dudes certainly didn't become punks. Shader Record Nerds aren't joiners. To see a world beyond Maple Shade was enough.

Which, as I think about it, is a very Shader way to explain things.

98.

Notes on Crack-Ups

I thought I knew how I wanted these Notes to end. I wanted to end with that scene from other memoirs, the one that appears in the third acts.

You know that scene. The memoirist sends an Insane or Eccentric Parent a copy of their manuscript, the one that tells their story. They meet at a coffee shop. The memoirist asks the Insane or Eccentric Parent if he or she had read the manuscript that tells their story.

"I did," the Insane or Eccentric Parent says. "And you know what? You got it *right*."

They embrace. Cue music.

It sounds cheesy, and it is. But that's how I wanted these Notes to end.

That's not how these Notes will end.

. . .

"Life, ten years ago," F. Scott Fitzgerald writes, "was largely a personal matter." What he had before him was "not the dish he had ordered for his forties." Fitzgerald was writing about his crack-up, his mental breakdown.

. . .

Here's a crack-up, one of my own. I'm out for drinks with a writer friend we'll call the Ambitious Poet with No Self-Doubt. "We should be putting together our selected collections by now," he says. "We're in mid-career. We need people to take notice of our work."

As the Ambitious Poet with No Self-Doubt says this, my hands shake a little. Then they shake a lot. I order a shot of whiskey. I pop a Valium I had stashed in my messenger bag for a couple years. I'm not sure what triggers my reaction, other than the thought that I can't talk about this.

But we do talk. We talk about writing and getting grants and not-getting grants, who publishes whom. I order another drink, pop another Valium. After a couple hours, I say goodbye to the Ambitious Poet with No Self-Doubt and get into my car to drive home.

I'm not drunk, not really, I say to myself. Just a little buzzed.

A couple blocks down, I feel woozy behind the wheel and pull over to take a rest. I drive into an empty parking lot next to an abandoned factory building. I guide the car up to the wall, very slowly, until the front bumper kisses it.

As soon as the bumper hits I punch the accelerator, pedal to the floor. The rear wheels scream on the tar. The back of the car shimmies back and forth.

"Bitterness is not far from death," Dante writes. Midway through my life I found myself bitter, not far from death, laying wheels in a darkened parking lot.

◆   ◆   ◆

Here's another crack-up, from November 2009. I am driving my Honda Fit across the empty interior of Pennsylvania to lecture at a college. My father has just had a stroke. Email and text messages forwarded from my sister—the sole ambassador from our side of the family—has increased levels of distress over our dad's health.

"This stroke is the big one," Meri says. It will require surgery. He needs to stay in the ICU until they can open him up. His alcohol intake and smoking needs to stop before anything can be done. "He's sneaking out to smoke Lucky Strikes," Meri says. "His spirits are way low. You know, maybe this time you should call."

I take down the hospital and room number, and resolve, for reasons I still can't explain, to keep driving along as my dad and I talk. I put the earpiece in and turn down the radio.

We say hello. He sounds tired. I tell him I am driving in the middle of Pennsylvania, on the way to a teaching job. This mention of Pennsylvania seems to lift his spirits up. "Remember what I said—once you get past Harrisburg, you're in America," he says.

His heart attack hurt, he tells me.

"I'd like to talk to you once in a while," he says. "I promise I won't say anything stupid."

We say goodbye.

·   ·   ·

Fourteen years before the conversation took place, I decided to break things off with my father. It seemed like I had no other choice: after he said disparaging "stupid things," about the ethnicity of my Jewish and Irish girlfriend, now my wife and mother of our children; after he stopped sending me Christmas presents; after he sent me a gun in the mail; after he never came back for funerals or weddings or births or graduations; after he flew on a trip to Germany to visit distant relatives named Nester, but not to visit his own children with the same name; after I realized he believed a lot of the stupid shit he talked about when I was a kid; after he seemed to not love me anymore.

I was wrong.

295

. . .

Fourteen years. If the time since I spoke to him were a boy, he'd be starting high school. His balls would be dropping. If it were a cat, it would be an old cat, like ours; it would sit on a radiator and stare at us, tired, hungry. It took 14 years for a man in India to dig a tunnel with a hammer and chisel so people in his village wouldn't have to walk 7 kilometers over a mountain; 14 years between the second and third Boston albums; 14 years to build two of the pyramids in Egypt; 14 years for Susan Lucci to win a daytime Emmy award.

. . .

My sister forwarded over an email that night.

"I spoke to my son," Dad told the doctors as he was wheeled away into surgery. "He called me."

Notes on an Afterword

January 1, 1992. I greeted the new year from a cold concrete floor on East 37th Street. The black drapes of Derek's apartment kept the place dark well into the morning, save for the red lights and random bleeps from a wall of electronics.

I had helped Derek deejay a New Year's Eve party. A bunch of Skidmore College students had rented a space on Jane Street in the Village. When the clock struck midnight, they ordered us to play Katrina and the Waves' hit, "Walking on Sunshine," three times in a row. We suspected cocaine was involved.

• • •

By our junior year, Derek had dropped out of Rutgers and moved to New York City. His company, Digital Ultra Sounds, promised the then-revolutionary all-CD, "all-digital" sets of music. As Digital Ultra Sounds' assistant DJ, my tasks included setting up two state-of-the-art Sony Discmans on top of small pillows to prevent them from skipping.

Derek called his place "The Studio" because it was an illegal sublet in a commercially zoned building. It really was a studio, though: in one corner he had set up a mixing board, speakers, microphones, and a set of electronic drums; in another, there were large plastic tubs of marijuana. Someday, Derek said, the next *Fear of a Black Planet* or *Ride the Lightning* will be recorded in his bathroom-less room in Murray Hill. Until then, he sold pot and deejayed parties.

I might sound like I am judging Derek, but the truth is that I was jealous of him. Derek was living the life. He helped around in a studio while the Fat Boys recorded their cover of "Wipeout." He played Sega against a Beastie Boy. He had even begun work as a male model. Before the party, we went downtown to lower Broadway and looked at a billboard above the V.I.M. jeans store. We looked up at a 20-foot-tall image of his likeness. The photographer had Derek stand and stare out heroically as two skinny models held onto his legs.

My last job was as a temp proofreader in Philadelphia, I thought to myself. Punk rock and hair metal were fading, Nirvana had the number one album, the golden age of rap was over, Freddie Mercury was dead. And all I accomplished was checking grammar on accounting reports. What was I going to do with my life?

Sitting stoned in Derek's apartment got old. Leonard, a poet who owned a bookstore in Philly, told me about the Poetry Project, which held an all-day marathon reading on New Year's Day. Anyone who's anyone in New York poetry came to read. Allen Ginsberg would be there, Leonard said, as well as hundreds of other real poets. I wanted to spend the day out on my own, to find my tribe, as hokey as it sounds. I wanted to spend the day as a poet in New York. I asked Derek how to get there.

"It must be on St. Mark's Place," he said. "Go out the door, make a left. Then make a left on Third Avenue. Keep going until you hit St. Mark's and make another left. St. Mark's Place is only two or three blocks long, so it should be there somewhere."[24]

.   .   .

I snaked beside the Queens Midtown Tunnel traffic on 37th Street and took a left turn downtown. Murray Hill is by no means scenic, but in my memory Third Avenue was the Champs Elysees. The bodegas and doorman buildings, the taxis in dormant midtown, the closed-up curry places on 29th, the large intersections at 23rd and 14th—all of it seemed part of my personal movie set.

.   .   .

I turned left on to St. Mark's Place and started to look for the words POETRY or PROJECT or anyone reciting a poem. Nothing. Halfway down the block, I started to get nervous.

Why did I go out into the cold only to get lost twenty blocks away? And why did I get stoned before doing this?

.   .   .

I spotted a building in the middle of the block, its bottom half painted white. Down a half flight, a group of people sat in folding chairs. Some held what looked like manuscripts on their laps. This must be the place, I thought. The New Year's Day Marathon Poetry Reading!

---

24 A couple things, especially if you already know the directions Derek just gave me were completely fucking wrong. First: the Internet wasn't around yet, so cut us both a break. Second: people from New Jersey don't bring maps to New York City. Jersey people think a city map comes with their brains, or appears there once they pass Exit 12. Or we just tell the cab drivers where to go. It's the Bridge and Tunnel Credo and we abide by it. Everyone I've ever met from the Midwest, for example, lands in Manhattan armed with maps, tour guides, tip sheet printouts on the cheapest beer or Indian food. Jersey people show up and ask other Jersey people. Or we tail Midwesterners.

The attendees were mostly older men, black guys and white hippies. This was the scene at most poetry readings. I found the first free folding chair and sat down and focused on the reading. Across from me, a man read his poem.

"I am now clean more than 60 days," he read. "I know I can make it this year. I know I can."

The poem seemed very pedestrian. And dull. So did the next one and the one after that. I soon realized that this was not The Poetry Project at St. Marks; it was in fact a center for people in recovery that happened to be located on St. Marks Place.[25] The poets were clients, drug addicts who were sharing writing with one another as they fought to stay sober.

I made myself a cup of coffee and dipped out onto St. Marks Place.

＊ ＊ ＊

I made it to the right place somehow. I sat on a pew in St. Mark's Church and warmed my hands and feet. "Everything becomes an allegory for me," Baudelaire writes. As I listened to each poet greet the new year, it felt as if everything had become an allegory for me, too. It felt as if each poem flew into the air and landed on my lap. It felt as if I had begun a new poem, one that was my very own.

---

25 This address, 19–25 St. Marks Place, was also the site of the Electric Circus discotheque, where Andy Warhol's Exploding Plastic Inevitable with the Velvet Underground happened in 1966.

Acknowledgments

First and foremost, this book is for my mother, my mom, Patti Little Nester Dudek McCabe.

◆ ◆ ◆

To everyone in my family: my sister Meri, Aunts Chrissy, Terry, and Dale, Uncles Tom, Bob, Mike, Kaz, my stepfather Bill, all my cousins, and my grandparents, the late Helen and Daniel Curtis Little. Your names may be different, but I love you all the same.

◆ ◆ ◆

I am beyond grateful to Jonathan Silverman at 99: The Press for his guidance and faith in this project, his mentoring and example-setting.

◆ ◆ ◆

Thank you to Thomas V. Hartmann for his invaluable support for this book, as well as his students in the Rosemont College's publishing class for their input and ideas: Laura Crockett, Amber Midgett, Hannah Walcher, Mara Delgado, Morgan Hawk, Brent Reif, Jen Murphy, Martha Nobles, and Jaime Schwender.

◆ ◆ ◆

Portions of *Shader* have appeared in the following publications, often in different form: *Indiana Review*, *The Morning News*, the *New York Times*, *n+1*, *Poetry Foundation*, *Freerange Nonfiction's*

Freshly Hatched, The Nervous Breakdown, Superstition Review, Hotel Amerika, Coldfront, Philadelphia Weekly, Albany Times Union, WAMC, and *Chicken Soup for the Soul: The Power of Forgiveness.* Thank you to those editors for their support. Their help and validation are deeply appreciated.

• • •

Much appreciation to those who have provided feedback on this manuscript over the years: Christopher Connelly, Josie Schoel, Alex Tunney, Brian Clements, Dwonna Naomi Goldstone, Dean Rader, Michael Gottlieb, Deborah Ager, Stephen Hunt, Anton Pasquill, Lina ramona Vitkauskas, Maggie Balistreri, and Mark Rhynsburger.

• • •

Thanks also to Richard Eoin Nash, Michael Costello, Jane Carman, Sara Lippmann, Buddy Beaudoin, Cristin O'Keefe Aptowicz, Keith Gessen, Katia Zorich, Chris Lee, Andrew Womack, Andy Ross, Chloe Caldwell, Eric Wybenga, Jill Ivey, M.E. Griffith, Ernest Hilbert, Mira Ptacin, Nita Noveno, Brad Listi, David Lazar, Adam McOmber, Sean H. Doyle, Carissa Halston, Brigitte Byrd, Bruce Covey, Hallie Goodman, Kate Sterlin, Thom Didato, Thomas Beller, Joanna Yas, Jen Hyde, Katie Vermilyea, Eric Schnorr, Dana Daidone, Dan Long, Brian Rhody, Aldo Naboa, Brendan Jemison, Jenny Taylor, Rita Soto, Michael McCann, Kevin DiNovis, Dara Dandrea-Gianotti, Keara Gianotti, Oran Gianotti, Sue Holmes, Sarah LaDuke, Marj Hahne, Afaa Michael Weaver, Donald Mull, Tony Abbate, Robert Andreano, Bobby Boyle, Bobby Ray Harris, Marty Franzen, Kim Oliver, Sam Preto, Katherine Davis, Ed Cook, Keith Thompson, Jim Cipolla, Bill Perkins, Karen Olt, Meri Olt, and Bill Roberts.

• • •

I'm grateful for a fellowship from The Center for Citizenship, Race, and Ethnicity Studies (CREST) at The College of Saint Rose for assistance and the time for the completion of this book. Thanks to John Williams-Searle and Andrew Ficili.

• • •

Thank you to all Shaders, past, present, and future. This is just one Shader's take, and while I own my own story, you own yours, too. This book is for you. Even if you beat me up.

• • •

In memory of my father, Michael Nester (1947-2013).

Notes on a Writerly Bio, Told in the Third Person

Daniel Nester is the author of *How to Be Inappropriate*, described as "a deeply funny collection of booger-flecked nonfiction" in *Time Out New York*. Nester's first two books, *God Save My Queen: A Tribute* and *God Save My Queen II: The Show Must Go On*, are collections on his obsession with the rock band Queen. A third, *The History of My World Tonight* (BlazeVOX, 2006), is a collection of pretty good poems. He is also editor of *The Incredible Sestina Anthology*. His writing has appeared in such places as the *New York Times*, *The Morning News*, *Salon*, *The Daily Beast*, *The Rumpus*, *McSweeney's Internet Tendency*, and the Poetry Foundation website, and anthologized in such collections as *Lost and Found*, *The Best American Poetry*, *The Best Creative Nonfiction*, *Third Rail: The Poetry of Rock and Roll*, and *Now Write! Nonfiction*. He is the former editor of the online journals *Unpleasant Event Schedule* and *La Petite Zine* and worked as Assistant Web Editor for Sestinas for *McSweeney's Internet Tendency*. Currently, he is an associate professor of English at The College of Saint Rose in Albany, N.Y., where he teaches writing. He lives in upstate New York with his wife and two daughters.